FriendRaising

Community Engagement Strategies for Boards Who Hate Fundraising but Love Making Friends

FriendRaising

*Community Engagement Strategies
for Boards Who Hate Fundraising
but Love Making Friends*

Published by:

Renaissance Press

4433 E. Broadway Blvd. Ste 202
Tucson, Arizona 85711 U.S.A.

Orders@Help4NonProfits.com
http://www.Help4NonProfits.com

Workbook Design and Artwork by Dimitri Petropolis

ISBN: 978-0-9714482-0-9

Library of Congress Control Number: 2006920098

 Renaissance Press • Tucson, Arizona

Make new friends, but keep the old.
One is silver and the other is gold.

Acknowledgments

It seems only right in a book about FriendRaising to celebrate the friends who have helped bring this book out of me. I hope you will bear with me as I thank them.

First, to the people all around the globe who spend their days and nights trying to make the world a better place - I am humbled to work with you all. I am especially grateful for the incredible international internet community that is Charity Channel (thank you, Steve, for making that possible). I learn far more from all of you than I could ever teach, and I thank you for letting me be part of the work you do.

To the Tucson community that helped birth the Southern Arizona Community Diaper Bank; to the Diaper Bank's director, Cheryl Smith, and each member of the Diaper Bank's board of directors; to the dedicated and passionate individuals in the Phoenix area who built and continue to nurture the Valley of the Sun Community Diaper Bank; to the thousands of friends who keep the mission of those Diaper Banks alive; and to every person who has dropped a package of diapers into a bin over the past dozen or so years, I am indebted to you for raising awareness of the issues affecting our most vulnerable residents, every single day. And I am personally grateful to each of you for the blessings I have received from the work we have done together.

To Steve, Mary and Kate Cortopassi, your willingness to share your home with me, giving me a place to hide away and write - that is a big reason a book like this is possible. And I owe special thanks to Nanette Pageau, Jane Savitt-Tennen, Kathie Driskell, Renata Rafferty and Dyan Petropolis, who patiently read various iterations of this manuscript, giving me valuable input, even when they thought they were not being very helpful. This is a different book than it started out to be, and that is because of them. They are on every page, and it is a better book because of that.

The Tapioca Gang saves my life pretty much every day. You guys know who you are, and you know how amazing it is that we have found each other. You are my family and my cheering squad and my butt-kickers, my source of horrible puns that no one should ever repeat (but we do anyway), and even an occasional source of breakfast. Thanks for sharing your wisdom, your whining and gossiping, your computer knowledge, the photos of your dogs, cats and kids. More than that, thanks to all of you for feeding and caring for my baby as she has journeyed forth into the world.

Debbie and Ray, Marty and Jeri, and my Mom and Dad have always been there for me and always will be, wherever each of you are right now. Nina and Max, you have my heart and you know it.

And finally, thanks to my family, who feeds my soul - to Nanette Pageau, who reflects me to myself, providing an always-present dose of clarity and wisdom and love; to Dyan, Mito and Derek Petropolis, who are proof that family is what you make it, and that life is not worth living if we aren't all laughing; and to my daughter, Lizzie Sam, whose passion for life and compassion for the world continue to be my inspiration. Lastly, my most special thanks to Dimitri Petropolis, my business partner and best friend, who has shared all the joys, all the agonies, and most importantly, who has made this book look gorgeous.

I cannot imagine life without all of you, and I am humbled and honored to have you by my side as the adventure continues. I cannot wait to see what comes next.

Disclaimer

Do not buy this book if you are looking for a book that will finally get your board to fundraise.

If you are looking for a magic pill to make your board raise money, you have two options:

① Buy a different book - one that will tell you what you want to hear.*

② Buy this book. Read it cover to cover. Share it with your board. And then decide if maybe this is a better way.

With that out of the way, let's get started.

---

* If you do find a book that will "make" your board fundraise, here is a second disclaimer - one for THAT book: It probably will not work. Has anything you have done so far really worked to get your board to fundraise? Do you think perhaps it is time to consider a different way of thinking?

Table of Contents

PART 1

Know Yourself First

STRATEGIES

PART 2

Making Friends

Matchmaking: Introducing Personal Friends to Your Organization

STRATEGIES

❖ **Meeting One on One**

❖ **Introducing Whole Groups to the Organization via Informal Board Member Parties**

Host an Event at Your Home

Birthday Parties

❖ **Introducing Whole Groups to the Organization via Organized On-Site Events**

Barn Raising (a.k.a. Volunteer Parties)

Focus Group Event

Annual Meeting Event

Part 2: Making Friends (continued)

Making New Friends

PART 3 Asking Friends for Help

STRATEGIES

PART 4 To Make a Friend, Be a Friend

AfterWords

Introduction

You've Got to Have Friends

As I am writing this book, songs come to mind. While love songs abound in our culture, many of the songs that stick around year after year are about friendship. Bette Midler belting out "You've Got to Have Friends." James Taylor doing Carole King's "You've Got a Friend." Andrew Gold's "Thank You for Being a Friend," that eventually became the theme song to the Golden Girls. Twenty or thirty years after the latest ode to love has come and gone, songs about friendship endure.

Look at television, the cultural touchstone of our age. Which shows last forever? The ones where the friendships are strong. In the U.S., "Friends" obviously comes to mind. So does "Will and Grace." During its run as one of the hottest shows ever, women admitted that more than coveting the shoes worn on "Sex and the City", they coveted the enduring and abiding "I'll always be here for you" friendship of those 4 women. Years after they have gone off the air, we smile to think of shows like "Cheers" and "M.A.S.H." and "Taxi". Around the world, the television shows that invite viewers to feel part of a group of friends rank high on the lists of favorites, year after year.

In my own life, my friends have been everything. What I have with my dear old friends makes life ok all the time. Making new friends is more fun than any activity I can think of. Learning about new people, seeing where and how we fit together, becoming part of their family as they become part of mine.

Friendship is supportive. It is inspiring. It is joyful.

Fundraising

A few years back, I approached a friend - one of the best fundraisers I know - and I asked her to teach me to ask for money for the Community Diaper Bank, the organization my business partner and I had founded. She looked at me as if I had grown another nose. "What are you talking about? You've raised hundreds of thousands of dollars. Everyone in town supports the Diaper Bank. Is this a joke?"

And I hung my head in confession. "Asking for money scares the life out of me."

The truth is I am not alone. Even in the best-selling guides to asking for money, the authors talk about how scary that effort can be. Yes, there are some people who feel comfortable asking for money, and there are others who learn to do it and eventually grow more comfortable with it.

But there are just as many Board Members, if not more, who would rather have a root canal than ask for money. For those people, being forced to ask for money brings on a unique form of stage fright.

Because nonprofits are under the impression that one of the primary roles of the board is to raise funds (it is not - the board's most critical role, first and foremost, is to lead, to govern), consultants continue to tell Board Members they will need to just get over it.

If we pictured instead telling all our Board Members that they needed to go on stage and speak before 500 people, consultants would never dream of telling their clients, "Just get over it; it's part of your job." But it is that same stage fright that disables many Board Members when they consider asking for funds. In addition, when it comes to asking for money from their friends, many of our friends are involved with their own causes. If we ask them for money, they will just ask us for money.

And in truth, how good is any of this for the long term health of our organizations? When we ask our personal friends for money, we know most will not become true friends of the organization, but will merely remain personal friends of a Board Member. When that Board Member is no longer around, will that friend still be a donor?

Equally important, the requirement that boards fundraise alienates many Board Members, making them feel inadequate, and keeping some good potential Board Members from joining boards in the first place.

So where does that leave us? It leaves us with a huge percentage of Board Members who hate to raise money, feeling pressured to do so or flat out not doing it. It leaves us with frustrated fundraising consultants and Executive Directors. It leaves us with prospective Board Members who do not join boards at all because they do not want to do fundraising. (We actually call one of our FriendRaising classes, "But I Don't Know Any Rich People!")

And when Board Members do raise money from their friends, often those friends stop giving when those Board Members stop asking - when they leave the board.

Perhaps instead of trying to get our boards to fundraise, it's time to start asking a different question altogether.

We've Got It All Wrong

Ask anyone which is more enduring, friendship or money, and you will find a direct correlation between how content or fulfilled that person is and his response. If money is more important to that person, he may have a nice car and a nice home, but he may also confess to feeling empty. On the other hand, if friendship is more important, while that person may struggle here or there and worry sometimes, he will likely look back at having lived a happy, fulfilled life. Those for whom friends are more important than money are often the ones whose families talk about them as always wearing a smile, even in the face of adversity.

A person who is rich in friends is indeed rich. A true friend will be there to dance when times are good, and will be there with both shoulders (for crying) and both arms outstretched (for helping) when times are bad. A true friend relishes sitting up late into the night, catching up when it has been way too long between visits. A true friend will help you move when you are finally heading into that dream home (in good times) or when your marriage crumbles (in bad times).

These are the relationships that make life worth living, the relationships that support us in every way.

So where is that component in our nonprofit organizations?

In my experience, nonprofits use the word "friends" in 2 ways:

1) We are advised that "fundraising is about relationship building." If we want money, then we had best be good about building strong relationships with our donors.

   This is the transactional view of friendship. "If you give us money, we will be your friend. If we think you will give us money, we will court you as our friend. If you fail to give us money, we will eventually stop calling you. The more money you give us, the more friendly we will be."

QUIZ QUESTION:

Does your organization have the same intimate relationship with your $10 and $15 donors as you do with your $1,000 donors? For your $10 donors, do you know if that gift is potentially MORE dear to them than the $1,000 gift is to that larger donor? Could it be that the $10 donor cares MORE about your organization than the $1,000 donor does?

2) The term "friend-raiser" has become almost a code-word for rationalizing a failed fundraising event. We have all heard it - the excuse for why we spend 6 months of staff and board and volunteer time on an event that provides a paltry profit once we have netted out the salaries of the staff and the goodwill and time of the board and volunteers. "Well the event isn't just a fundraiser. It's a friend-raiser," could be the rallying cry of failed fundraising events everywhere.

This is the rationalizing view of friendship. "If we don't make our primary goal - money - we can always just say we were looking for friends."

QUIZ QUESTION:

If you find yourself using the fall-back position that your fundraising event is also a "friend-raiser", how many new friends does the event really raise? Do those people become true friends, or are they just new faces at that one event? Have you ever measured to see if there is a way to more effectively raise friends? More friends? Truer friends? Friends who are not only there because their company bought a table, but because they care about your cause?

Programs the Community Would Not Let Die

A while back I was talking about the Diaper Bank we founded with the representative of a major foundation in our community. He was complaining about the number of organizations that approach him for funds, many of whom tell him, "You have to fund us - you are our last hope. Without this money, we will have to close our doors."

My friend vented his frustrations. "If they haven't proven to the community that they are doing something necessary; if they have not brought the community along with them and made the community part of what they are doing - well then maybe they *should* close their doors!"

And then he focused on the Diaper Bank. "You couldn't kill the Diaper Bank now if you wanted to. The community would not let you."

The key to creating ongoing support lies in my friend's words. How do we build programs the community would not let die?

And the answer is simple: If you build strong relationships between your mission and the community that benefits from that mission - building real friends who really care - that community of friends will not let your mission die. Those friends, your very community, will become your army of support.

Building an Army of Friendship and Support: It's All About Relationships

Picture yourself at a cocktail party. You are introduced to someone you have never met before. In the few moments you have together, this new acquaintance tells you a bit about himself; you tell a bit about yourself. You are interested in learning more about the work he does, about his life. And it is at that moment that your new acquaintance says, "You know a bit about me now. You seem to like me. Would you give me $100?"

Is this any more absurd than how we view "prospective donors"? When we see everyone as a prospective source of money, we ignore what it might mean to have that person as a real friend.

In our own lives, our friends care about us personally, care that life goes well for us, and care about the things we care about. Our true friends help when our kids are born and when our parents grow old. True friends know us so well that we do not have to put on airs - they enjoy just having us around, and we feel the same. Real friends would never let anything bad happen to us, and they will go out of their way to make sure good things come our way.

The same holds true for the friends we make for our organizations. Real friends will volunteer; they will arrange for speaking gigs; they will provide in-kind gifts; they will introduce you to others who might want to be your friends as well. They will sit on advisory panels regarding your mission and counsel you on your programs. And yes, they will donate cash.

I don't know about you, but I would rather have that sort of friend than a mere donor any day.

We humans are so capable of getting what we aim for. When we ask for money, we raise money. But when we focus on raising money, we are always wishing we had more friends.

When we aim for friend- ship, we build relationships. We ask for friendship, and we get all the

amazing things that come with friendship. Money becomes just one of those many gifts.

So in answer to my friend's shock that I had raised so much money while being intimidated to ask for money, here is what I had learned without knowing I had learned it: To build programs the community will not let die, we need to stop focusing on money. We need to start building an army of friends, an army of support. Those friendships are the key to building sustainable efforts to improve the quality of life in our communities.

Who We Are

Dimitri Petropolis and I have been consulting to nonprofits as Help 4 NonProfits & Tribes since 1993. For the first few years of our consulting practice, we used the same tools most other nonprofit consultants use. The results met our clients' expectations, and through referrals for a job-well-done, our business grew.

But after a few years, we became frustrated. While the results of our work met our clients' expectations, those same results did not meet our own expectations. We had chosen this line of work in the first place because we wanted to use our skills to help make our world a better place. Yet the classic "nonprofit organizational development" tools - strategic planning, fund development planning, marketing planning, board development, etc. - were achieving neither large-scale community impact nor organizational sustainability for the nonprofits we worked with.

In 1997, that frustration led to the commitment to reinvent those nonprofit tools, to ensure nonprofits had everything they needed to make our communities better places to live. We dedicated ourselves to re-thinking all our assumptions. Why did we believe what we believed? What made an approach the "right" or "wrong" approach? And we spent years developing new tools and methodologies, testing those approaches with clients and seminar attendees, going back to the drawing board to tweak some more, and then re-testing again as we went along.

But That Is Not the Whole Story

There is a second half to this story. And that half starts way back when we celebrated surviving our 1st year in business by creating a cute and funky holiday giving effort - a Diaper Drive to help two organizations in our hometown of Tucson, Arizona.

By the time the years rolled by and we were at the point of questioning our consulting tools, our annual December Diaper Drive had become so large, it had outgrown our capacity to keep running it as our personal act of philanthropy. We set out to create a Diaper Bank, to ensure this much-needed commodity would be provided year round. After looking around to learn how other Diaper Banks worked, we soon found we were about to form the first Diaper Bank in the country, and perhaps in the world.

As if running a business and starting a nonprofit were not enough to keep us busy (not to mention our two families with young kids), the publicity the Diaper Bank received in those early years caused a ripple we had not counted on - demand for the same service in other communities around the world. And that led to our heading up the road to the big city - Phoenix - to build a second diaper bank, the Valley of the Sun Community Diaper Bank.

Community-Driven

It has now been many years since the epiphany that there had to be a way for nonprofit organizations to provide more lasting benefit to their communities. Over those years, we developed and adjusted our tools and approaches with clients and workshop attendees. We used those tools to create and then operate 2 brand-new and now growing organizations. We tested and retested.

And after all those years, as we stepped back to see what had evolved, it became clear that we were no longer working on "new tools." What had developed was instead a comprehensive and overarching approach to the way nonprofits do everything they do - a whole new model. It is a model that addresses the question of community impact from the inside out, focusing organizations on accountability for the mission, sustainability of that mission, and most importantly, substantial improvement to the quality of life in our communities.

These are *not* business approaches adapted for the nonprofit world. Instead, these approaches were developed specifically for the realities of life inside organizations whose sole purpose is to make the community a better place to live. They are approaches that focus on both the end result - community impact - and the means to achieve that impact.

We call it the Community-Driven Approach to running nonprofit organizations.

Community-Driven means just that - that boards focus their primary accountability on providing impact for the community. That we stop talking about why we cannot provide that impact, and that we instead focus on ensuring we have the means so we *can* provide that impact. That we stop seeking short term funds at the expense of long term ability to provide the mission. That we engage the community in everything we do, because we are more powerful when we do our work together than in a vacuum. And that working with the community means building long term relationships based on mutual benefit and trust - real friendships between those individuals and the missions of our organizations.

As Jim Bostic, Executive Director of the Nepperhan Community Center in Yonkers, New York told us after flying 3,000 miles to attend one of our workshops, "This is a far more intelligent way to run our agency."

For more information about these Community-Driven approaches, please see the resources in the AfterWords of this book. In the meantime, know that the strategies in this workbook all stem from that model. They are all aimed at making your organization more Community-Driven, seeing both short term survival and long term sustainability, all within the context of long term improvement to your community's quality of life.

All of Which is a Long Way of Telling You What This Book Is About

This book is intended, first and foremost, as a guide to FriendRaising, a Community Engagement approach for boards to connect the community they love with the mission they are passionate about. We have two goals in writing this book.

First, it is our goal that your community become so deeply integrated into the fabric of your organization's mission and vision, that the community would never let your efforts die. Because one look at your organizational chart will show you that your board is the link between your organization and the community to whom you are accountable, there is no group more logical to build that army of friends than your board.

Which leads to the second goal - putting to rest the ridiculous notion that the most important part of being on a board is fundraising, and vanquishing the myth that the best Board Members are those who bring in the most money. Board membership is about governing and leading, and a big part of that is what is often called the role of Ambassador - providing the link between the organization and the community you serve. And so our second goal in writing this book is that, after all these years of feeling inadequate, every Board Member will finally feel he or she has found a meaningful way to support the heart of the organization's mission, building friendships that provide all sorts of benefit, rather than just focusing on money.

To accomplish this second goal, we have presented a smorgasbord of possibilities that both board and staff can happily use to make friends and engage them to support your work.

To accomplish that first goal, though - the goal of deep community engagement - you will find that this book presents a whole different way of seeing your organization's position in the community than most of us are used to. Most organizations are accustomed to focusing inward, trying to survive. When we turn that focus outward, though, we see that we are really all in this together - that it is not "our organization" in here and "the community" out there. By creating a Community Engagement approach to building sustainability for your mission, you will begin to work with all those individuals who make up your community, seeing them as part of the fabric of your organization, because each of their lives is somehow affected by the work you are doing. When we use FriendRaising to engage those community members as real friends, we are linking arms to create substantially more impact in our communities.

This new way of being grows slowly in some, and comes as a jolt of sudden enlightenment to others. But the more friends you raise, and the more you begin to see how easy it is to bring the community into your organization while bringing your organization out to the community, the more you will see that this approach to sustainability simply makes sense. And that is because friends will help with everything. They will volunteer and they will make connections. They will give advice about the mission and the community, and yes, you can even ask them for all kinds of stuff, including money.

This book is not intended as a primer on Community Engagement for your whole organization - that book would be quite different, as it would focus on aspects that are touched upon only lightly here. So then, what is this book about? It is a guide for boards, because boards desperately need a different approach to their ambassadorial role. It is about making friends, keeping friends, asking friends for help, and being a friend yourself, all with the intent that the community will indeed be a better place when we realize we are all in this together.

Work Your Board Will Be Happy to Do

As you will see from the strategies in this book, FriendRaising activities are the kinds of efforts every Board Member will be excited to participate in. When we stop telling Board Members they must raise funds, and we provide them instead with a variety of ways to help build relationships that will support the organization's mission at its core, your Board Members will begin to make friends everywhere they go.

This approach is energizing, as it asks Board Members to tap into the abundance of resources your organization's friends do have, rather than the large piles of money they may not have.

By taking this approach, you will never again have to cajole, because your Board Members will want to help.

They will want to help because the efforts are not intimidating. Board Members never have to worry if it is the right time, or the right approach, when all they are asking for is friendship.

They will want to help because the efforts are all focused around the mission, the reason they have joined your board in the first place.

But mostly, Board Members will want to help because making friends is, quite simply, fun.

Our Board Doesn't Know Enough!

When we teach these approaches in our sustainability workshops, participants will often approach us privately, embarrassed to tell us, "Our board doesn't know enough to do many of these activities." That may be true for your board as well.

That is why #1 of all these strategies is to get to know your organization better. If your Board Members do not know the things they need to know to accomplish these strategies, the impact of that lack of knowledge goes far beyond their ability to help provide support. It impacts their ability to be accountable for what the organization is and does - their ability to govern effectively and proactively overall.

The side benefit of this learning is therefore obvious: Once your Board Members know enough about the organization to do these activities, they will be far more capable leaders as well.

Using This Book

This book is intended to take your board through the various stages of preparedness for engaging with the community. It is a workbook, and we hope you will use it as such, writing in it and scribbling ideas in the margins. To make the book more user-friendly, copies of the brainstorming forms can be found in PDF format via links in the AfterWords.

Part One will help your board prepare to take on the task of engagement. What do we need to know before we get started?

Part Two focuses on making friends. How do we engage our personal friends with our organization's work? How do we meet entirely new friends?

Part Three looks at the types of groups found in every community - businesses, schools, congregations, and the like. That section then provides pages of strategies for engaging each of those groups to become part of your army of friends.

And lastly, in Part Four, we will bring it all back to the reminder that to make a friend, we must first be a friend ourselves. Here you will find the motherly admonition that prior to heading out to ask others for help, each Board Member should be engaging in as many of the activities in this book as they will be asking others to engage in. We cannot ask others to do what we are not willing to do ourselves.

As you read through the many strategies that follow, we have a few words of advice.

First, pace yourselves. Don't dive in, trying to accomplish all these ideas at once, or you will quickly burn out. Choose one or two strategies that make sense for your whole board, and perhaps one or two additional activities that each Board Member might want to do on his/her own as well. But attempting to do all these activities at once will make you exhausted - and that is certainly not the point!

Second, adapt what you find here. Not all activities in this book will work for every board or every Board Member. Use the ones that make sense for you, while adapting the essence of some of the others to see if you can create a way that works for your board and accomplishes the same result. And we are excited to hear about the new ideas you come up with as you use these strategies to jump start your own thinking.

Third, once you have tried one or two activities and seen how easy they are to accomplish, consider creating a Friendraising / Community Engagement Committee, who can help develop and implement a Friendraising / Community Engagement plan. This item is addressed more completely on page 22.

Lastly, in the words of the old Nike ads, just do it. Try something, anything. Go for it and let your successes energize you to do more.

About the Examples

One last explanation before we dive in. Originally, the examples throughout the book came from a broad variety of sources. Because we have been using this approach with clients and workshop attendees for a long time, we had a range of stories to share.

But upon reviewing an early draft of the manuscript, Jane Tennen, Director of New York University's George Heyman Center for Philanthropy & Fundraising, said, "You originally learned how to do all this by actually doing it with the Diaper Bank. You learned it the hard way and can now share it from that perspective. Instead of trying to be even-handed, why not just tell the story of how two crazy people succeeded in starting and sustaining a nonprofit?!"

So we took Jane's advice. The narrative thread throughout the book is the story of how our tiny private philanthropic effort not only became the world's first Diaper Bank, but became a prime example of how Community-Driven an organization can be at its core. There is barely an approach in this book that we have not tried, tweaked, and re-tried with the Diaper Bank, as we basked in the ability to use our own "baby" to test our theories and new approaches. (There may be a situation or two where a client's or colleague's work is so exemplary that we cannot help but use their example, but we have tried to stick to our own as much as possible.)

As you see how we have used these strategies, we hope these examples will inspire you to try them for yourselves.

My best friend is the one who brings out the best in me.

Henry Ford

PART

Know Yourself First

This above all: to thine own self be true, And it must follow, as the night the day, Thou canst not then be false to any man.

William Shakespeare, Hamlet

STEP 1 Know Yourself First

Before we can make friends, we must know ourselves first. From there, the rest flows naturally.

And while the steps in this section will pave the way for all the FriendRaising activities in this book, these steps will, first and foremost, make you better Board Members. Conscious knowledge of this basic information will increase your ability to effectively lead your organization.

This section includes the following strategies:

#1 Know Your Organization's Story

#2 Know Your Organization's Core Values

#3 Know Your Organization's Real Needs

#4 Know Your Plan

#5 Know Who You Know

#6 Know the Rules of Friendship

STRATEGY

#1 | Know Your Organization's Story

As we have worked with organizations to implement the strategies in this book, Board Members have often approached us privately, confessing, "I don't think I know enough about the organization to do these activities." As it is in real life, it is hard to make a true friend until you know yourself first.

If your Board Members feel they do not know enough to represent the organization in most of these activities, then your first step should be the development of an ongoing board education program. The reason for that program goes beyond simply having the information to participate in the activities in this book. In truth, if you do not know enough about the organization to do these activities, you do not know enough to govern effectively. So the creation of an ongoing board education program will serve both purposes - allow the board to govern more consciously, and turn your Board Members into better FriendRaisers for the organization!

At the annual retreat of a neighborhood social services center, the Executive Director had planned to devote the lunch hour to updating the board about the center's programs. What was intended as an update, however, was brand new information to most of the Board Members present, regardless of their tenure with the organization.

Board Members were shocked. "If we don't know such a basic thing as our programs, what else don't we know?" And they spent the rest of the afternoon discussing just that.

When a new Board Member mentioned feeling lost not knowing everyone's name, the group voted to require name tags at every meeting, to smooth the transition for new Board Members and for guests.

When a veteran Board Member confessed to not understanding the financials, that comment unleashed such a flood of me-too's that the board decided to create a financial education program for all Board Members.

They all wanted a tour. And they voted to set aside 15 minutes of every board meeting for learning about the programs, so they could make more informed decisions.

By day's end, they had crafted a combined program for board orientation and continuing board improvement. That afternoon brought this board together in ways no team-building exercise ever could have. And it put them on the road to responsible governance.

Brainstorm Sheet:

❖ Know Your Organization's Story

To determine what your board's education program should include, have Board Members answer the following question:

As you read through this book, what information do you feel you are lacking? What information would you need before you could execute most (all?) the strategies in this book?

_____
_____
_____
_____
_____
_____
_____
_____
_____

And have the CEO answer:

What areas of the organization do you feel the board does not understand well enough to execute most of the strategies in this book?

_____
_____
_____
_____
_____
_____
_____
_____

These will be the topics for your board's education program.

#2 | Know Your Organization's Core Values

Before we can talk about representing your organization to the community at large, it is important that we talk for a moment about core values and ethics. And while the buzzwords of "accountability for the money," and "business ethics," seem to be bandied about with greater and greater frequency, the issue of core values and ethics go far beyond those limited terms. Your organization's values will be at the heart of the friendships you form.

Values guide the way your organization does its work. In addition to the obvious issues of fundraising and internal financial controls, your values guide how the organization does all its work, from the way you treat personnel to the way you make decisions that affect the service clients and patrons receive.

If you are going to build friendships, those friends will want to know what you stand for. And the more clear you can be about just what "talk" you want to "walk," the easier you will make it for folks to march along with you.

Overall Values

The issues of organizational values address the most critical questions about your mission: What are we about at our core? What is important to our organization, that we want to model to the rest of the world? What is at the basis of the decisions we make? What beliefs will guide our behaviors? When we are asking a friend to believe in our organization, what are we really asking him to believe in?

From the answers to these and other similar questions, you will be on your way to creating a Working Credo - a single sheet that tells the world what ethics they can expect to encounter when dealing with your organization. As you can see from the credo on the next page, this is a useful tool for sharing with prospective employees, prospective Board Members, prospective collaborative partners, prospective friends and donors - anyone who may want to support the work your organization is doing in any way.

Values and Friendraising

As you dive into the strategies in this book, meeting new friends and asking them for help, are there lines you will not cross? Those lines are indicators of your values.

    If a friend offers to print a banner for your event for free, is it ok if their business's logo is on the banner? What if the business is a beer distributor, and your organization is a sobriety group - is it still ok?

These types of questions arise all the time. And the answers are what will define who you are and who your friends are.

- Your organization is fighting child labor overseas. A local retailer sells items made by child labor. The retailer's employees want to volunteer at your highly public event, all wearing T-shirts from their company. Is that ok?
- Your organization is an environmental group addressing energy issues. The local SUV dealership offers to donate vehicles to help move your office. Is that ok?

There is no right or wrong answer to these questions. It all depends on your organization's values - the things the organization stands for. The important thing to note, though, is that the time to determine your values regarding these issues is *not* when there is a pot of money on the table, or when your lease expires in 3 days and you need to move NOW! The time to determine what your organization believes at its core is long before you need to put those values to the test.

Once you have developed a statement of your organization's values, you will be able to hand that policy / credo to any prospective friend of the organization, and he/she will know up front the values for which your organization stands.

In these times of corporate scandal, as you head out to meet new friends, these are the types of questions you will want to know you can answer, before they are asked.

SAMPLE WORKING CREDO

Southern™ Arizona Community Diaper Bank

Working Credo

When making decisions at the Diaper Bank, the board, staff and volunteers will be accountable for and conscious of the following:

☑ The best decision will be the decision that provides the best end result for the highest number of our partners, the clients they serve, the issues they address, and the future of our community.

☑ The core reason the Diaper Bank exists is to lessen the current effects of poverty and crisis, while working simultaneously to eliminate the root causes of poverty and crisis in the future. Today's decisions will therefore be made in the context of both today and tomorrow, asking the question, "How will this decision affect the future of our organization AND the future of our community?"

☑ All parties to any decision will be treated with respect, dignity, compassion, grace, integrity, honesty and humanity.

☑ Our message must be positive, that we CAN make change. With a passionate optimistic message, we can change minds and move mountains.

☑ We can accomplish significant change if the whole community works together, focusing ALL the community's varied resources towards improving our community's quality of life. All the community must share ownership of our problems and our solutions.

Brainstorm Sheet: _____

❖ Know Your Organization's Core Values

To create your working credo, the following questions may be helpful prompts:

What words do you think those who participate in your programs - patrons, clients, customers, participants - use to describe your organization? **And what words do you want them to use when they speak about your organization?**

_____

_____

_____

_____

_____

What words would your employees use to describe their feelings about their supervisors? About the board? About the whole organization? How do _former_ employees talk about the organization? **And what words do you want them to use when speaking about the organization?**

_____

_____

_____

_____

_____

What words would supporters use to describe your organization (cash donors, in-kind donors, volunteers, advisors)? How would they describe the effectiveness of your organization's impact on the community? How would they describe the integrity with which you manage both the mission and the means to attain that mission (personnel, facilities, money, etc.)? **And what words do you want those supporters to use when speaking about you?**

_____

_____

_____

_____

_____

#3 | Know Your Organization's Real Needs

As you begin to engage the community, integrating new friends into the heart and soul of what makes both your organization *and* the community strong, you will realize the immense resources your community has to offer. As your friends begin to offer those resources to you, it will be important to understand the real needs of your organization, to be ready when those opportunities arise.

What do we mean by real needs? The needs beyond money. When we think, "We need money," that is all we get. When we think, "We need to build a successful program. That means we first need advice and wisdom, then staff and volunteers, facilities, equipment, outreach efforts..." - that is what we get! The more you look beyond money to consider what your programs really need to remain strong, the more you will be able to tap on the assets and resources that already exist in your community. That is what sustainability is all about.

AT THE DIAPER BANK

Knowing the Diaper Bank's Real Needs Leads to a Whole New Way of Operating

Starting a brand new organization, with a mission that had never before been addressed, provided the Diaper Bank with creative license - there was no "this is how it's always been done" to follow. We spent many months prior to opening our doors talking with / asking questions of community leaders, to determine the Diaper Bank's best chances for survival.

From those discussions, we realized we were facing a critical decision in how to structure this new organization. We could form a stand-alone organization - gather a board, find a building that could warehouse the 2 million diapers needed annually for low income babies, disabled and elderly folks, and hire enough staff to distribute all those diapers to people in need.

Or we could identify the functional needs of the Diaper Bank, and share those functions with others in the community who already had those resources in place.

We chose the latter. We started by listing everything we would need to serve our mission. Caseworkers. Tools for getting the word out. A warehouse. Trucks to pick up diapers from collection points. We even noted the need for advice about the program we were creating.

Then, next to each item, we listed who in town already had those things. And we played matchmaker.

Here are just 2 examples of what we found.

Caseworkers
The Diaper Bank could have hired one or more caseworkers, to determine who would qualify for diapers. Or we could work through existing agencies who already screen clients.

We chose to share that workload with organizations already doing the work.

continued ☞

AT THE DIAPER BANK *continued*

The reason for this decision went beyond just cost savings - it went directly to the heart of the mission. First, families would not have to requalify for yet another program, and go to yet another location to get diapers. Secondly, though, if individuals were in need of diapers, they likely would need other things as well. By having the diapers distributed by agencies who could help families in more holistic ways, those families would receive more of what they need, to get back on their feet.

Talk about a way to engage friends! Had we hired our own caseworkers, we never would have been sharing a mission with 75 other agencies- agencies as diverse as a substance abuse treatment center, a teen pregnancy program, a job training facility for the developmentally disabled, a crisis shelter for abused babies, the city's subsidized elder-living facilities, the Salvation Army - the list goes on and on.

Had we not been partnering with those agencies directly, it is likely we would have seen them as competition. Instead, because we share their mission, they have all become friends. These friends send volunteers; they donate cash; they give program and advocacy advice; they house our board meetings in their conference rooms, updating our board on their individual missions. Had we chosen to go it alone, we would have missed out on this opportunity to create something far larger and more powerful than just another nonprofit agency. Together, we are one huge army with one overarching mission - to make life better for those in need, and to work to make our community a place where fewer people live in need.

Warehousing

When we budgeted the expenses to receive, inventory, store and distribute 2 million diapers per year, the estimate was approximately $50,000 annually. That included warehouse rent, utilities / insurance, and personnel costs for an experienced warehouse person, not to mention the capital costs of racks and forklifts, etc. Setting up and operating a warehousing operation is not cheap!

Instead of doing this function ourselves, we sent a request to the nonprofits in our community. Do you have some excess space and staff who can do the job? Could we figure out a way to work together?

We were shocked at how many organizations responded, all wanting to help.

The group that has now been the Diaper Bank's warehousing partner for 5 years is an organization that provides vocational training to disabled adults. With a huge warehouse already in place - racks, forklifts and 20 foot ceilings - and staff already trained, the Beacon Group uses the diapers to train the developmentally disabled with warehousing skills. And what might have cost $50,000 per year or more has cost only $15,000 per year. This is the win-win of a great friendship!

By listing out your real needs, you begin to see that it is really not about money. It is about understanding those needs so your friends can help to meet them. And in the process, you will find you are beginning to spread the roots of ownership of your mission throughout the community - a strong start to building programs the community would not let die, simply because so many friends are part of keeping it alive.

Brainstorm Sheet:

❖ Know Your Organization's Real Needs

What Does Your Organization Need, and What Do You Need It For?
Are you developing a new program? Looking for ongoing support for existing programs? Expanding a program? The resources needed for those programs will each be different. List the programs that will need resources of any kind in the coming year.

_____
_____
_____
_____
_____

To operate those programs day-to-day, what resources does each program need? Personnel / Volunteers? Facility expansion or a new facility? Equipment? Furniture? Professional assistance such as marketing, legal, accounting advice? What else? List the resource needs of each program.

_____
_____
_____
_____
_____

In addition to the nuts-and-bolts of furniture and volunteers, what kinds of advocacy support do your programs need, to make a bigger and bigger difference? Public speaking? Help connecting with people of influence over your issue, such as legislators? What do you need to get your issues of concern in front of those who can help?

_____
_____
_____
_____
_____

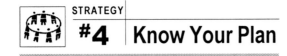

STRATEGY
#4 | Know Your Plan

There are two ways to use a book like this one. Both approaches work. One works better.

The first approach is to choose an activity here or there that sounds appealing, and to try it, see if it works, then perhaps try another. You might have each Board Member choose an activity that seems appealing to him or her. You might even include, as part of your board's letter of commitment (You do have a letter of commitment, don't you?), that each Board Member adopt at least one approach from this book, as his/her way of connecting with the community throughout the year. We guarantee that if you use this approach, you will make new friends and increase support for your organization's mission.

However, there is another approach that can raise even more support. And that approach is to combine the strategies you choose into a cohesive Community Engagement / FriendRaising plan.

A Community Engagement / FriendRaising plan will look in part like a fundraising plan, and in part like a marketing plan. But then it will eliminate / change some of the elements of those plans, adding others of its own. That is because the goal of this plan is *not* just money (fundraising), and *not* just awareness (marketing). The goal of the Community Engagement plan will be to interact with as many different portions of the community as possible, to build that army of friends who will help make your mission work in every way imaginable.

By engaging the community, you will raise volunteers; you will raise in-kind support; you will raise political support; you will raise awareness of the issues you are trying to address; you will raise the level of benefit the community receives from your programs; and you will raise money - all at the same time!

The steps in creating this plan could encompass a whole book in itself. But the basic steps are the same as any planning process.

Step 1: Determine the goals of the plan. The goals of the plan should include the community engagement needs from all your organization's other plans over the coming year or two - however long your planning horizon is.

You may want to add another goal, in addition to those from other plans: to simply increase the number of friends your organization can count on. (It helps to quantify that, for example, "We want to have met and gotten to know 50 new friends this year" or "500 new friends this year" or "5 new friends this year.")

Step 2: For each of those goals, determine who in your community needs to be engaged to ensure that goal can be achieved. Consider the approach taught by advocacy guru Nancy Amidei - look for not just the "likely suspects" but the "unlikely suspects" as well. If you are recycling computers to give to families with little means, does the Sierra Club have a stake in keeping those old computers out of the landfill? You bet they do!

You might start by listing broad categories of the types of people you want to engage. But once those categories are listed, name names to attach to those categories. You cannot befriend a category; for friendship, you need a live human being. (Some of the efforts in this book will help you to find more and more names to add to the list.)

Step 3: Determine who on that list you already know. Using the activities in this book, determine how you will approach them, and how you might engage them.

Step 4: Determine who is left on the list, to get to know. Using the activities in this book, determine how you will approach them, and how you might engage them.

Step 5: Prioritize those activities. There are only so many hours in a day, and only so many people on your board. Determine which of those activities is most likely to accomplish what you need to accomplish, and focus on those. Be objective as you weigh the activities against each other. Do what will get you the best results.

Step 6: Create an implementation plan: Determine what steps you will take to accomplish the goal(s) for each activity you choose. Who will do what, and when? Be specific. "By next Tuesday, Jamie will write a letter," and etc. You can calendar a whole year's worth of activities in this fashion.

As you create this implementation plan, build measurement into that plan, so you can easily monitor your progress. How many people will be contacted, by when? And how will the board monitor to ensure that work is being done?

Step 7: Get out there and do it, and monitor your progress. Having measurable objectives makes it easy to monitor progress towards achieving your goals. A plan is not worth anything if it is not implemented and adjusted along the way. And the only way the board can ensure the plan is doing what you need it to do is by monitoring that plan at every meeting, as part of the reporting items the board reviews.

Step 8: Maintain those relationships. The single most important step in every one of the activities in your plan will be what happens when that activity is done. Know ahead of time who will be in charge of maintaining that friendship on behalf of the organization. As you look at the strategies in this book, you will see that many of them call for follow-up. After that follow-up, though, what will be next? How will you be sure that 6 months and 12 months and 36 months from now, that relationship has not been forgotten in the effort to meet new friends? That song every Girl Scout knows to her grave could not be more true: "Make new friends, but keep the old. One is silver, and the other's gold."

Brainstorm Sheet: ▬▬▬▬

❖ Know Your Plan

What will be the goals of your Community Engagement Plan? List the Community Engagement components of your organization's other plans, plus your separate FriendRaising goals.

_____

_____

_____

_____

_____

Which "likely suspects" need to be engaged, to achieve each of those goals?

_____

_____

_____

_____

_____

Which "unlikely suspects" need to be engaged, to achieve each of those goals?

_____

_____

_____

_____

Which activities will you use to engage each of those individuals with your organization's work?

_____

_____

_____

_____

STRATEGY #5 | **Know Who You Know**

When we ask Board Members to raise funds, it is not unusual to hear the refrain, "But I don't know any rich people - I don't run in those circles!" However, when you are building an army of friends, you do not need to know rich people. The friends you already know are just the friends your organization needs!

Before embarking on the activities in this book, therefore, it will be helpful for each of your Board Members to develop a Life List - the list of all the people they know.

Your Life List is simple to create. And as you look at the results when you are done, you may be surprised at just how many contacts and friends you do know!

Your Life List will be the basis for many of the other activities in this book. In addition, though, often the mere act of listing these people sparks ideas about ways for board members and their friends to provide assistance to the organization.

So let's get to work. Start with your holiday card list, or your business Rolodex, and list everyone you know. Use the forms on the following pages to spark your thinking, and you will quickly realize you know more people than you think.

List at least **2** people you know personally, who belong to and attend meetings of a Civic Club such as Rotary or the Chamber of Commerce (preferably in different clubs).

☑ _____

☑ _____

List at least **2** people you know personally, who are decision-makers within their company - who are department heads, etc.

☑ _____

☑ _____

List at least **2** people you know personally, who work for the government (City, County, State, Federal, School District, etc.).

☑ _____

☑ _____

List at least **2** people you know personally, who work at a large company, in any capacity - entry-level employee or manager or anyone in between.

☑ _____

☑ _____

List at least **2** people you know personally, who are elected officials (City, County, State, Federal, School Board, etc.)

☑ _____

☑ _____

List at least **2** people you know personally, who work in Public Safety (police, fire)

☑ _____

☑ _____

List at least **2** people you know personally, who have kids in a local school.

☑ _____

☑ _____

List at least **2** people you know personally, whose kids are active in a club, scouts, sports, after school activity, etc.

☑ _____

☑ _____

List at least **2** people you know personally, who attend religious services regularly / are involved in their congregation.

☑ _____

☑ _____

List at least **2** people you know personally, who perform personal services for you or your family (hairdresser, pool company, attorney, accountant, plumber, mechanic).

☑ _____

☑ _____

List at least **2** people you know personally, who are teachers or decision makers at local schools.

☑ _____

☑ _____

List at least **2** people you know who are involved in their neighborhood association / homeowners association.

☑ _____

☑ _____

List at least **2** people you know personally, who own a small company.

☑ _____

☑ _____

List at least **2** people you know personally, who are active members of a union, or members of a club (knitting club, book club), or a sports team (bowling league, softball league).

☑ _____

☑ _____

List at least **2** people you know personally, who paid to attend a charity function of any type (gala, golf tournament, theater night, etc.) in the past year. (Perhaps you ran into them at the event?)

☑ _____

☑ _____

List at least **2** people you know personally, who seem to know everyone in town - whether through their business, their church, just their gregarious nature, etc.

☑ _____

☑ _____

List at least **2** people you know personally, who are on the board of other nonprofits in your community, or who are Executive Directors or other key employees of a nonprofit in your community.

☑ _____

☑ _____

List at least **2** people you know personally, who you believe have given at least $25 to at least one charity in the past year.

☑ _____

☑ _____

List at least **2** people you know personally, who work for another nonprofit organization.

☑ _____

☑ _____

List at least **2** people you know personally, who volunteer (including sitting on the board) at another nonprofit organization.

☑ _____

☑ _____

List at least **2** people you know personally, who have led really interesting lives.

☑ _____

☑ _____

List the people on your holiday card list, who don't fall into any of the other categories

☑ _____

☑ _____

☑ _____

☑ _____

☑ _____

☑ _____

☑ _____

☑ _____

Specific to Your Organization:

List categories that are specific to your organization's needs. Then have your board members list the people they know in those categories.

For example, if your mission is related to health, you might seek 2 people who work in a hospital, 2 people in medical administration, 2 people who work in alternative medicine. If your mission is related to youth sports, you might seek 2 people who work in recreational fields, or 2 people who are volunteers with youth sports.

List at least **2** people you know personally, who

_____.

☑ _____

☑ _____

List at least **2** people you know personally, who

_____.

☑ _____

☑ _____

Specific to your Organization: *(continued)*

List at least **2** people you know personally, who

_____.

☑ _____

☑ _____

List at least **2** people you know personally, who

_____.

☑ _____

☑ _____

List at least **2** people you know personally, who

_____.

☑ _____

☑ _____

List at least **2** people you know personally, who

_____.

☑ _____

☑ _____

"All those lives we touch, and the lives those people touch, and then the lives they touch - the whole community is part of our family. Our job is to make sure they know that!"

Workshop Attendee at Help 4 NonProfits' Sustainability Workshop

STRATEGY
#6 | ## Know the Rules of Friendship

My mom is 81 years old. Her best friend passed away a few years ago. Eileen and my mom had been friends for almost 60 years.

They met in their late teens, working as secretaries in New York City's garment district in the early 1940's. Meeting at the elevator, they realized they were both walking to the same subway. From the subway, they realized they were both getting off at 183rd Street. They were both young and cute and sassy, ending the day laughing on the way home. They were neighbors, and they became friends.

They married within a few years of each other, both finding men who would be by their sides until parted by death. It had never occurred to them that their husbands would not get along, but in fact that is what happened. It never occurred to them that they would move to what might as well be different parts of the universe - suburbs at opposing ends of the city, with a 2 hour drive if there was no traffic. But that is what happened as well.

Yet they remained as close as if they still lived within blocks of each other.

When Eileen was diagnosed with Multiple Sclerosis in her late 20's, and through the ups and downs of the years she battled her illness, Eileen and my mom were together. When my mother lost her first child early in her marriage, and then later, through the sudden loss of the husband she adored, Eileen and my mom were together. Through the all-consuming days of raising their families, the distance between them, the trials of their lives - Eileen and my mom were together.

After my dad died, my mom made the hardest decision of her life - to move 3,000 miles from the place she had called home for 65 years, to the desert in Tucson to be near my family. And within just a few years, finding it more and more difficult to maneuver her wheelchair in the snow and slush, Eileen and her husband moved 2 blocks away from my mom.

After all those years, they were once again neighbors and friends.

To the end, they could talk about anything. To the end, they understood each other. They trusted each other, depended on each other, were generous and kind to each other, protective and accepting of each other, of their kids and grandkids. And to the end, they continued to laugh - Eileen, so debilitated by 45 years of her illness, and my mom, nearing 80 years old herself. When they were together, they remained as cute and sassy as those days when they had first met, talking about boys and giggling on the way home from work.

That is friendship.

That is what this book is about.

Friendship is about kindness and generosity and compassion. It is about reciprocity, about that 2-way street of dependability, trust, nurturing. It is about feeling protective, wanting to ensure no harm comes to your friend.

Friendship is not about what we get, but what we give. It is about gratitude, graciously giving thanks for the gift of that friendship.

Friendship is about the third entity that is created when we are together - not "me" and "you", but the "us" that is more powerful than simply 2 individuals coming together.

Friendship rejoices when there are reasons to celebrate - both the big things and the little things (especially the little things). And friendship feels real pain when one of those friends is suffering.

Friends know each other better than anyone else in the world. When spouses are also friends, when parents and children are also friends, outsiders can tell just by watching them together. There is joy surrounding them.

Friendship can grow slowly and consistently over time, or it can hit you between the eyes the moment you meet, as if you have known each other all your lives. We cannot force it either way, but fast or slow, when it is right, we both know it.

Friends share advice, wisdom, and yes, gossip. Friends trust that what their friend says is true. They acknowledge each others' flaws and do not let foolish things get in the way of their friendship.

Long term friends find joy in watching each other change and grow over time.

It is not surprising the producers of the television show "Friends" chose the theme song they did, because if there is any theme that sums up friendship, it is those words: "I'll be there for you."

That is what this book is about. When you engage with members of your community in real friendship - not that euphemism for wanting their money, but true friendship - your community will never let your mission die. And that is because your friends will be part of that "us" you have created - that thing that is bigger than each of you separately could ever be - the us of a community working together to build a better place to live.

You will no longer be just neighbors. You will be real friends.

You know your organization's programs.

You know your needs, your values, your contacts.

You have a plan
and
you know the rules of true friendship.

Let's start putting it all together
to create and engage
your organization's army of friends!

The making of friends, who are real friends, is the best token we have of a man's success in life.

Edward Everett Hale

PART

2

Making Friends

Blessed are they who have the gift of making friends, for it is one of God's best gifts. It involves many things, but above all, the power of going out of one's self, and appreciating whatever is noble and loving in another.

Thomas Hughes

MATCHMAKING: Introducing Personal Friends to Your Organization

There comes that mysterious meeting in life when someone acknowledges who we are and what we can be, igniting the circuits of our highest potential.

Rusty Berkus

MATCHMAKING:
Introducing Personal Friends to Your Organization

As simple as it sounds, the first step in engaging the community with your organization's work will be to meet people. Just as it is in our "real" lives, sometimes we meet new friends at work, or at a party, or at school. And sometimes we are introduced by a mutual friend.

Your board, as the connecting link between the organization and the community, is that "mutual friend." Looking at your Life List, it may be surprising how many people you know who are prospective friends for your organization.

This section addresses that first step - and often the most awkward one. How do you introduce these two parties? And how do you do so in a way that builds the trust that will be the foundation of that relationship?

If you have ever fixed up two friends on a date, you know how awkward this can be. Even if you've just had two friends you thought should know each other - no dating, just friends - that first meeting is stressful. You have told Mary about Susan for years, and you really think they would get along. You finally get them together over lunch. Sometimes the pressure of that moment is like stage fright! What to say, how to keep the conversation rolling - and what if they really don't like each other? Then it will not only be awkward at lunch, but all you have told them about each other - oh, how will you save face?

And then 3 minutes into lunch, you know your instincts were right. The two of them take over, and you might as well not be there.

That is what this section is all about: Creating the environment where your two friends - the organization, and whomever it is you want to introduce to the organization - will begin to get to know each other.

The approaches in this section include:

- ❖ **Meeting One on One**
- ❖ **Meeting at Informal Board Member Parties**
- ❖ **Meeting at Organized Group Events**

Once you have introduced individuals to your organization, it will be important for the organization to have concrete plans for nurturing those new friendships, to develop them into long-term fruitful relationships for both your new friends and your organization. In this section, however, we will focus on the role of Board Members in first making those introductions.

And remember: introducing does ***not*** mean asking for something. If we were introducing 2 people to each other, just so they would know each other and become friends, neither would have his/her hand out.

You can make more friends in two months by becoming interested in other people than you can in two years by trying to get other people interested in you.

Dale Carnegie

❖ Meeting One on One

Meeting one on one is a wonderful way to take personal time for friends to get to know each other. Whether it is over lunch, in an office, on a tour - the ability to spend quality time with a new friend is golden.

The approaches on the following pages focus on that intimate setting, introducing one friend at a time to your organization. These approaches can be great first steps, and they can also be great follow-ups to the group events described in other portions of this book.

The One-on-One Strategies

#7	Personal Advocacy
#8	Using an Introductory Mailing (and Follow-up) to Build Relationships
#9	Breakfast with Friends
#10	Community Sleuthing
#11	Hosting a Tour

STRATEGY
#7 | Personal Advocacy

Let's start at the beginning - with each individual Board Member. It will be a lot easier for your board as a whole to connect with the community if each of your Board Members has been converted into a personal advocate for your organization's mission. And all that takes is simply being you and telling your own story.

At cocktail parties, at the supermarket, and just about any time I run into friends or meet new acquaintances, the answer to, "How are you? What have you been up to?" will invariably include something about diapers. These are not long lectures, but just a sentence about what's new and exciting at the Diaper Bank. We are always surprised at how many people are intrigued to know more.

What is Personal Advocacy?

The most effective way to communicate your organization's message is to speak one on one, person to person, in real conversation about your organization. If our goal is to establish real friendships, isn't this what friendship is all about?

Each of your Board Members should become a personal advocate for your organization, taking every opportunity to talk about the work and the mission, with anyone who will listen.

What is the Goal of Personal Advocacy?

The goal of this strategy lies at the very heart of building friendships for your organization - the very heart of community engagement. Everything your organization needs to do its work, from input on its programs to construction of a new building, is furthered by turning each of your Board Members into a personal advocate for your mission.

The benefits of this strategy will go beyond simply making that connection. By increasing awareness in this way, you will be helping to elevate the level of discussion of important issues in your community.

And equally as important, you will be walking proof that this is a board that is excited to do its work. And that enthusiasm is one the best tools there is for recruiting new energetic Board Members.

Who is the Target of this Strategy?

Anyone who will listen. Seriously.

How to Become a Personal Advocate

You are at a party, and the host introduces you to someone new. "This is John. He works at ABC Corporation." And as you extend your hand, you add, "Well actually, the most exciting thing I'm doing these days is not at ABC. I'm on the board of the Children's Group, and the work we are doing there is what has really got me excited!"

Or you are at your networking group, and you are given 1 minute to brag about something. "Last week, at our board meeting of the Children's Group, we decided to move forward on a project that is so exciting!"

As an individual Board Member, you can talk about the things that resonate with you personally - why you got involved with this group in the first place.

If your board decides to use this approach aggressively, you might create a list of "Talking Points" - the things you want to stress as you have the opportunity to talk with the people in your life. The goals of your marketing / outreach plan are the best place to start with this, as they will outline the things the organization wants to communicate over the coming year.

What is the Role of the Board Member in this Strategy?

The role of the Board Member in this strategy is simple:

1) Know your organization.

2) Talk about it whenever you have the chance.

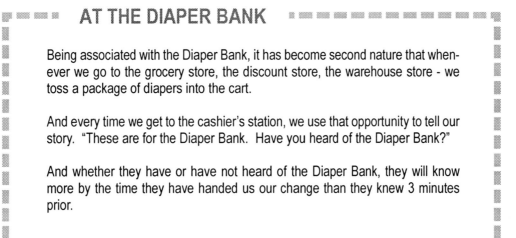

AT THE DIAPER BANK

Being associated with the Diaper Bank, it has become second nature that whenever we go to the grocery store, the discount store, the warehouse store - we toss a package of diapers into the cart.

And every time we get to the cashier's station, we use that opportunity to tell our story. "These are for the Diaper Bank. Have you heard of the Diaper Bank?"

And whether they have or have not heard of the Diaper Bank, they will know more by the time they have handed us our change than they knew 3 minutes prior.

STRATEGY #8 | **Using an Introductory Mailing to Build Relationships**

In the Diaper Bank's early days, there was no mailing list aside from our Life Lists. So once or twice a year, we would find an article that related to the Diaper Bank's work, and we would send a copy of that article to our friends. Once the issue was welfare reform. Another time it was about health care costs. It never takes much to relate what we read in the paper to the Diaper Bank's mission of fighting poverty.

When we sent the article, we would attach a quick note, letting them know why we had sent it. Because the effort was personal, a large percentage would reply with a call or a note of their own, or at least mention it when we saw them again. This quickly became a favorite way to start the conversation.

What is an Introductory Mailing?

Unlike a mass mailing - the impersonal fundraising letter we often throw away without even opening it - there is nothing impersonal about this mailing. Nor is it an appeal for funds.

The introductory mailing is instead just what the name implies - a great way to introduce the organization, as you begin to build long-term relationships between those you know and the cause you care about.

The key to this mailing is twofold:

    1) It sends information in a non-threatening, not-asking-for-anything way, and

    2) You will follow up personally after the mailing is sent.

What is the Goal of this Introductory Mailing?

If you are anything like most people, when you looked up from creating your Life List, you were surprised to see how many people you know who might, in some way, be interested in the work your organization is doing. The goal of this introductory mailing is therefore to create an easy way to introduce your organization to all those people in your life.

The important part of the goal comes from the follow-up to the mailing. By engaging friends first with an informal and informative mailing, and then following up, you are laying the groundwork for that friendship to take root.

Who Will Be the Target of the Introductory Mailing?

This strategy will apply to everyone on your Life List, as well as anyone else you have met through other efforts in this book. You may want to send the letters in batches, as the key to this effort is follow-up, and it will be hard for your Board Members to follow up with 30 or 40 people at once.

How to Use an Introductory Mailing (with Follow-up) to Help Build Those Relationships

The first step in your quest to build those relationships will be a mailing that asks for nothing but your friends' attention and perhaps some time to talk, to get their advice - to begin to build that friendship. Even if these are people you have known for years, to your organization, they are brand new friends.

Here is a simple way to get started with the people on your list.

    1) If you have not done so already, provide the organization with contact information for each of the people on your Life List.

2) Have your ED find a news clipping (or an editorial someone from your organization has written) or another pertinent, well-written piece that relates to the issues of importance to your organization. It is important that this be a third-party piece, and not just your regular newsletter. That layer of objectivity makes a big difference when it comes to credibility for this particular approach, as it shows that it is not just those inside your organization who think this is important.

3) You will be sending a copy of that article to each of the people on your list. (Again, you may want to spread the mailing out over a few months, to ensure you have time to follow up.) The mailing will include the following:

   ✓ The article

   ✓ A sticky-note from you. The note will be personal, asking for **nothing but their attention and perhaps their time**. For example: "I'm on the board of the Animal Lovers Group, and I'm really excited about what we are doing. I'd love to tell you about it and pick your brain for ideas. Can we have coffee and talk about it?"

   ✓ That's all.

You will **not** include a donation envelope. And you will **not** ask for anything but their time and their attention to a cause that is important to you.

   • "I'd love to give you a tour."

   • "I'd love to pick your brain about a project we are doing. Can I give you a call?"

   • "I'd love to have coffee and see if you have any ideas."

   • Or even simply, "I want you to be aware of this because it is so important."

4) The key to this effort is not merely sending the letter, but being sure you follow up. Without the follow-up, this effort will only temporarily raise awareness. And while that awareness has value, a bit of follow-up can convert that "awareness" piece into an introduction to a real friendship.

As follow-up, you will likely want to do one or two of the other activities in this book. As you have that cup of coffee, take that tour, or simply have that phone call, let your friend know about what the organization is doing, and ask for his/her ideas. Together you will begin to see how your friend might fit in. Does she have a child at school? Perhaps she belongs to Civitan or Soroptimist? Is she part of an employee group at work? Is she active in her congregation?

If your conversation goes the way most of these conversations go, you and your friend will likely start to get ideas about how their child in school, their Civitan or Soroptimist group, their employee group, their congregation, etc. can help attain your organization's goals.

The key will be to simply generate ideas together. Once you start the conversation, you will quickly see those connections almost happen on their own, (especially if you use a sleuthing approach - asking questions - as you will see in Strategy #10). That is why it is so valuable to extend the invitation by asking to pick your friend's brain!

5) Fold these individuals into your organization's ongoing direct mail campaign, making sure to write a personal note when future mailings are sent. This will be part of the ongoing follow-up that comes with maintaining that new friendship.

Remember - support comes from building relationships - ***not*** with you, but with the organization. Start slowly, take your time, and encourage folks to determine how they can best assist in whatever way makes sense for them - their time, their ideas, and yes, perhaps their money. These first steps - the introductory mailing with personal follow-up - will pave the way to engaging more and more friends in your mission.

What is the Role of the Board Member in this Strategy?

This is almost entirely a board activity. The Board Member may get clerical support from the organization, and some of your follow-up activities will likely involve staff members. But the rest of this activity - gathering the list of contacts, writing the hand-written notes, doing the follow-up - that is all reliant on your Board Members. And remember to pace yourself, as follow-up is the key. If you are one of those people who knows many many people, your list may require that you dedicate yourself to connecting with everyone on that list throughout the course of your whole board term. This is not a race. The quality of those friendships will count far more than the speed at which you send those letters.

STRATEGY
#9 | Breakfast with Friends

Steve Nill, founder and CEO of Charity Channel, insists (albeit somewhat tongue in cheek) that one of the best routes to organizational sustainability is through the smart use of breakfast. Never underestimate the opportunity to talk one-on-one over breakfast or lunch, about the great work your organization is doing. (And don't forget to pick up the tab!)

What is Breakfast with Friends?

If Strategy #7 turned your Board Members into personal advocates for your mission, this strategy takes that advocacy a step further. By taking time to deliberately engage your friends, talking about the work your organization does and sharing a cup of coffee, you will be introducing the organization to people with whom you already have a personal relationship, bringing them into the fold.

What is the Goal of this Strategy?

The goal of this strategy is twofold:
1) To share information about the organization in a way that will engage your friend, and
2) To find out what part of the organization's work your friend might be interested in pursuing further.

That's all. Again, this is about building a relationship, engaging your friend with the work your organization does. And we are not going to start this relationship with our hand out asking for money!

Who Will Be the Target of this Strategy?

This strategy will target anyone on your Life List with whom you would feel comfortable just having breakfast or lunch and telling about your organization.

How to do "Breakfast with Friends"

Before heading out to breakfast or lunch, decide what 2-3 key points you want to share with this person, both to inform your friend, and to learn from him or her - what observations does he/she have? The key points could be your organization's goals for the year or a new exciting project you are starting. But whatever they are, aim to tie your points to your friends' interests, and to ask for their input. Then make that part of the invitation. "I know you are involved in _____. I would really appreciate your thoughts on something similar our organization is doing..."

Because the goal of this effort is to share information as well as to listen to your friends' ideas and areas of interest, we recommend using the buddy system for these meals. Pairs of Board Members together, or teaming a Board Member with the CEO or other knowledgeable staff person, can make sure you have all the information you need to answer questions and to get multiple perspectives about the work you do. This is also a great strategy for new Board Members to learn the ropes from more seasoned Board Members, accompanying that Board Member for one of these meetings.

Bring along the organization's brochure, but refrain from bringing a whole packet of stuff. This is an introductory breakfast, not a study session!

Over breakfast, tell your friend about the organization's work. Tell about what excites you the most. Share common stories, interests. Tell him why you wanted to share this information with him in particular. Ask what about the organization interests him. Encourage him to ask questions. Encourage him to tour the facility. Encourage him to get involved, in whatever way makes sense. And yes, in all seriousness, unless your friend absolutely insists, pick up the tab!

Follow-Up

Follow up with a thank you note, and keep your friend on notice the next time there is an event where he can get more involved, perhaps a volunteer event where the two of you can work side by side. Again, the ongoing follow-up, by the Board Member _and_ the organization, is critical to maintaining a real relationship with this new friend.

Make it Easy to Track Information

It is important to track pertinent details about your breakfast, to be sure you can provide appropriate follow-up information to this new friend. Keeping this information in your organization's database is a big part of that tracking.

To make that tracking task easier, you might want to create a form that helps you note each friend's interests, specific things he/she mentioned, etc. The form should assist you to remember what to send them as follow up, but it should also be something you can hand to a staff person when your breakfast is over, so the staff can be sure all that information is entered into your organization's database. It would be a shame to have all this great information existing only in the memories of the people at the breakfast table, or on scraps of paper stuffed in the back of your Daytimer or PDA!

Have this form ready as you make your initial call, in the event your friend cannot make it to breakfast, but is willing to take a few moments to chat on the phone.

What is the Role of the Board Member in this Strategy?

This strategy is probably the most personal of all the strategies in this book, and, as such, almost the whole effort is up to the Board Member - making the invitation, making sure you have a knowledgeable companion (if that is not you), treating for breakfast, following up. The goal is that your friend eventually forms a relationship with the organization, rather than with you. But for this first time, it is up to you to make that connection.

AT THE DIAPER BANK

The Diaper Bank's board of directors has set "lunching" into policy. Each Board Member at the Diaper Bank is required to introduce 2 people to the organization via lunch or breakfast per year. And just as the board president is the one who gently reminds Board Members of their annual obligation to donate to the organization, the board president also gently reminds Board Members of their obligation to "lunch."

At the Diaper Bank, that obligation shows up in 2 places one might not otherwise expect to see it.

1) The Board Member letter of commitment includes the obligation to introduce 2 new friends to the organization via lunch or breakfast every year.

2) The board attendance matrix shows not only who missed what meeting and whether or not a Board Member has provided his/her annual donation, but also whether that Board Member has fulfilled the annual "lunch" obligation! *

*For more information about both these tools, head to the AfterWords

---

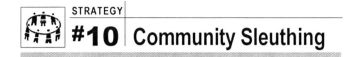

STRATEGY
#10 | Community Sleuthing

Perhaps because consultants learn to ask more than we tell, and to listen more than we talk, we love this strategy. We learn, we gain supporters, we find connections, and most of all, we get buy-in that lasts forever - all key components to FriendRaising. We credit Community Sleuthing with both the founding and the continuing success of Tucson's Diaper Bank.

More importantly, though, we owe it to Community Sleuthing that we were able to open the second Diaper Bank in the Phoenix area at all. By the time the ribbon was cut in Phoenix, there was both start-up public relations sponsorship and a year's start-up funding in place. And there was also enough community support to allow Phoenix's Diaper Bank to be created and operated from the very beginning almost entirely by Phoenicians - all in a community where we knew only a handful of people to start out!

From our experience, Community Sleuthing is the best way to engage the whole community in your cause, one person at a time. As our kids would say, Sleuthing rules!

What is Community Sleuthing?

We all know what a sleuth is - the detective who tracks down all the information he/she can find about the question at hand. That is exactly the essence of Community Sleuthing - asking people for their ideas, their thoughts, their perspectives. Community Sleuthing connects you directly with community members, providing you with their insights and support at the same time.

It is all done by simply telling your story, asking questions, and listening to the responses.

Community Sleuthing starts with the premise that "You never know." You never know what people know, what their experience has been, who they know, how they can help. People in your community have incredible wisdom to share. And the best way to find out what they know and what they think is to ask!

This strategy is therefore all about tapping into these incredible people, and seeing how their wisdom can help your organization. The great part is that by doing that sleuthing work - just asking those questions and listening to the answers - you will be accomplishing a variety of goals, all at the same time.

Once you learn to be a good sleuth, you will find this is a great approach to use at breakfasts, on a tour, or in many other circumstances where you are introducing your organization to a new friend.

What Is the Goal of Community Sleuthing?

Community Sleuthing will accomplish many goals at once. It is hard to emphasize how powerful a tool this seemingly innocuous effort can be.

★ **The Opportunity to Expand Your Thinking:** The information you receive from your Community Sleuthing efforts can help breathe new life into old programs, and can bring a well-rounded perspective to new programs. This speaks to the heart of an organization that is truly engaged with the community. In the course of these meetings, you will receive outside insights into:
  • Demand for your service
  • Others doing what you are considering doing
  • Potential collaborative partners
  • New ideas, issues and approaches you had not considered
  • Feedback regarding the way you have been doing your existing work
  • Whatever else is important and relevant to the work you are doing!

★ **The Opportunity for Direct One-On-One Connection with Your Mission:** Before you can ask your sleuthing questions, you will need to provide some background for those questions. That means you will have the opportunity to succinctly tell your story in your own words. Instead of counting on a brochure or public speaking gig, you will be briefly sharing your own insights into your programs and goals, one-on-one in a comfortable setting.

★ **The Opportunity to Generate Buy-in for Your Mission:** By approaching folks for their knowledge, and then following up periodically to let them know you are still thinking about the things they told you (or perhaps implementing their ideas), you are bringing them into your organization's family. You are showing them that they are not outsiders; they are part of a trusted team of advisors. A piece of them is alive in your organization!

★ **The Opportunity to Build New Connections:** Dust off that list of people you have always wished you could get in front of. Since all you will be asking for is information, there is no reason you cannot call the Mayor, the State Legislator, the town philanthropist, and ask for their wisdom. You will be surprised how many "yes" responses you get to your request for just 20 minutes of their time and their advice. And once people start referring you to others, you have the ideal door-opener: "Joe said you know everything there is to know about _____. Can we meet for just 20 minutes? We have some things we are trying to learn more about."

★ **The Opportunity to Build an Army of Supporters:** No matter how many individuals you meet using this approach, all those people will be well on their way to becoming friends of the organization. They will have learned about your program through your own words, and by giving you their input, they will feel a sense of commitment to the work you are doing.

In essence, by learning to "Sleuth," you will be learning to turn just one conversation into a deeply engaging encounter.

Who Should We Target for this Strategy?
While this strategy could apply to anyone on your Life List, this is a particularly good approach for
- Elected officials: People in elected office often come into contact with more people in a day than you might meet all month. They will be a great source of both information and contacts.
- Individuals who seem to know everyone: These people tend to know who is doing what, and that may translate into their connecting the dots in ways that might never have occurred to you on your own.
- People who have led interesting lives: It is not by accident that these people have led interesting lives. They have a vibrance, an energy, an ability to make things happen around them - and with all that comes wisdom to share with your organization.

In addition, you will want to add others to the Sleuthing list - those in your community you would simply love to get to know. Lastly, though, after you have done this once or twice, you will likely want to incorporate a "sleuthing approach" when you are breakfasting or touring friends around your site.

How to Do Community Sleuthing
Being a good sleuth is easy and enjoyable. It takes only one skill: the ability to listen.

1) Call for an appointment. Let the person you are calling know you are not on a fundraising mission - you are looking for information, not money. "I am working on a project and I could use some guidance. Do you have just 20 minutes for me to ask for your thoughts and ideas about what we are trying to do?"

2) Visit with them. Present what you are considering doing (or your existing program), and ask pointed questions about that work. Ask for their ideas, their insights, their wisdom. And then be quiet and take notes as you listen to their answers.

3) Listen more than you talk, and ask more than you answer. Do not argue, and do not jump at the chance to say, "But we already do that!" You are there to learn, not to persuade! Keeping quiet is the hardest part of being a good sleuth.

4) Before you leave, get 2 things:

  ① Permission to call him/her again if you have additional questions. (Getting permission to call again gives you instant feedback.)

  ② The names of 2 other people they think you should talk with.

5) When you are done, follow up with a thank you note, and offer to tour them through the facility. (Before assuming they are too busy, ask - you never know!)

6) Put this new friend's contact information into your contact management database, and make sure to have the notes from your meeting typed into that database as well.

7) Follow up with the individuals they refer you to, using the same approach.

After you have "sleuthed" someone and followed up with a thank you note, be sure future newsletters and other mailings include a special personal note, thanking them again for their insights, and perhaps updating them. Having the notes from your meeting in your organization's database will allow these follow-up functions to be more easily turned over to staff members, turning this one-time meeting into a life-long relationship.

And finally, keep each person posted on whatever project you discussed with him, especially the points that interested him. A short note saying, "Just keeping you posted on our progress!" is a great way to build on that initial meeting, especially if you can remind him of his suggestions and show how you have incorporated them into your thinking. As with the other strategies in this section, the introduction must be seen simply as Step 1 in the building of an ongoing relationship between your organization's mission and this new friend.

> ## SAMPLE SLEUTHING QUESTIONS
>
> Have you heard anything about the issues our organization addresses?
> - Do you know if there is demand for this service, that is not being met?
>
> Do you know of anyone doing something similar to what we are doing?
> - What do you know about their program?
> - Do you know someone at that program, with whom I might speak?
>
> We want this program to help improve the quality of life in our community.
> - Do you have thoughts about how we could create more impact?
> - How can we be as effective as possible?
>
> Is there anything you think we might have missed?
>
> Are there issues or approaches you would suggest we include?

What is the Role of the Board Member in this Strategy?

There are a variety of roles a Board Member can take in this effort.

- At minimum, every Board Member should connect the organization with people from their lists, setting up the appointments and sitting with the ED or knowledgeable staff member at these appointments. These could be breakfast appointments or a quick 20 minutes in someone's office - whatever works best for them.

- Board Members with extensive knowledge of the organization might choose to "fly solo" by meeting with community members individually and reporting back to the Executive Director. Provide the ED with notes from the meeting, which can then be followed up upon and entered into the database.

BIRTH OF A DIAPER BANK

When it came time to expand the Diaper Bank into other parts of Arizona, we knew there was more we did not know than we did know. The one guiding philosophy was that the Diaper Bank had to be owned by the community, and not by us "outsiders."

There was a balance to be struck, though. Without us outsiders, there would be no Diaper Bank, as we knew the need, we had the passion to connect the need to action, and we knew how to do it collaboratively, economically. We also had the credibility - we had already done it, quite successfully.

So we took out our Life Lists, and we started to make calls.

From the economic development conferences we had attended several years prior in conjunction with our work in Native American communities, we had met the Economic Development Director of one of the cities surrounding Phoenix. We called Brian and asked if we could just pick his brain about the community.

Brian included the Community Relations Director for that city in our conversation. And as we asked our questions about the need in the community, and the services that were already trying to meet that need, Sally started to brainstorm about other people who should hear about this, who might have different information for us.

She connected us with one of the staff in the Community Relations office at the Arizona Republic, the state's largest newspaper. The connection from Sally made our call less of a cold call, and Diana was happy to meet with us. We asked her the same questions we had asked Brian and Sally, talking about the same issues - child abuse, elder issues, issues surrounding the disabled.

Diana got excited about what we were doing, and introduced us to her boss, Gene D'Adamo, the head of Community Relations for the Arizona Republic. Gene's reputation precedes him in the Phoenix metro area, having dedicated his life to helping those in need. His time is well guarded, and had we cold-called him, we can only guess what our success rate would have been.

But coming through folks who knew folks - well, within a few months, the state's largest newspaper - the Arizona Republic - had offered to sponsor the first ever diaper drive in the Valley, providing free ads and more importantly, unbelievable instant credibility.

Using Community Sleuthing in the Phoenix area, we were also able to find this brand new Diaper Bank a $75,000 start-up grant from the Nina Mason Pulliam Charitable Trust. Sleuthing can be credited with the Diaper Bank's acquiring a free year of public relations as the annual pro bono client of BJ Communications. More importantly, thanks to Community Sleuthing, representatives from over 50 area agencies worked together for a year to build the Valley's Diaper Bank.

Clearly, Community Sleuthing showed the fallacy in the thought, "We don't know anyone powerful." In Phoenix, we not only did not know anyone powerful - we hardly knew anyone at all! The proof was in the pudding, though. Community Sleuthing proved we knew everyone we needed to know.

Note from a Convert:

We have always insisted that Community Sleuthing is hands-down one of the most powerful, energizing, most productive and least utilized approaches nonprofits have at their disposal. It costs nothing more than time, and it pays back that investment in more benefit than you can imagine.

But we also know it sounds - well - perhaps silly? Perhaps hokey? When we talk about sleuthing in workshops, we always get the same response: It's so simple. What's the big deal?

So we thought we would share the real words of someone who has used it. Gail Melone of Arizona's Healthy Mothers Healthy Babies Coalition told this story to the attendees at one of our workshops.

"Hildy suggested this to me some months back, when we were first starting up. And I have to admit, when she first suggested it, I thought it sounded really lame. But after talking to ten people about our program, I couldn't believe how it worked! We got information and buy-in and ideas - it's amazing. As hokey as this sounds, you really need to try this!"

STRATEGY
#11 | Hosting a Tour

A one-on-one tour of your facility is a powerful way to not just tell your story, but show your story! And while the thought of a tour musters images of kids playing in a playground, or beautiful gardens or art work to show off, all the Diaper Bank has ever had to show is a warehouse with racks of diapers - nothing much different from a walk down the diaper aisle at Target. But we always have a story to tell. And that is all we have ever needed.

What is a Tour?
No matter what your organization does, or how "boring" you might think your facilities are, there is nothing like a tour of the operations to connect people to the mission. Some organizations lend themselves easily to a tour - a zoo, an environmental group, a crisis nursery, an arts collaborative.

But if your organization does counseling, or legal aid, or educational enrichment - the kinds of activities that do not require much more than an office - the "tour" concept applies to you as well. And that is because a "tour" can just as easily be a tour of the mind.

Tours can be done in groups, but they are also very effective when done with one individual at a time, allowing for deeper dialogue about the subjects that are of interest to that particular person.

What is the Goal of this Strategy?
This strategy is the poster child for the "free sample" approach - don't tell them, show them! The goal of this strategy is to create an opportunity to go beyond simply telling your story. With this strategy, you will *show* your story to someone you want to become a friend, and you will show them by inviting them into your organization's home.

Who to Invite?
This strategy could apply to virtually everyone on your Life List. It will also apply to those you meet through other activities in this book, as well as those you meet in the course of your organization's mission work. A tour is often the perfect way to begin nurturing those relationships.

How Does a Tour Work (Especially If Our Facility Is Just Offices)?
When the suggestion of giving tours is made to boards, often they think, "This is easy - I'll get a few of my friends and show them around!" Soon those Board Members find it is not as easy as all that, simply because few individuals have time in their day to take a tour simply for the sake of taking a tour.

Therefore, your approach should be simultaneously honest and enticing. Here is one approach. We encourage you to think of others.

1) Make the tour about <u>them</u>. Tell your new friend why you specifically want to take him or her on a tour. Why him? Why her?

   "I've been thinking about your membership in Rotary. I'm not sure exactly what the fit would be, but I'd like to talk to you about how we might work more closely with some of the members of your Rotary. Could you meet me at our facility to talk, and I could show you around?"

   If you prefer to be more vague, you will still keep the focus on <u>them</u>. "You know I have been involved with the XYZ Group. I'd really like you to see what this place is all about and <u>get some of your thoughts</u>. Could you meet me at the facility to talk, and I could show you around?" You want their thoughts and ideas. "Why them?" is because you respect <u>them</u>.

2) On the day of the tour, you and your friend (or friends) will be joined by the Executive Director or another staff person or volunteer who is knowledgeable about the organization. Let the ED lead the tour and answer questions. (Side benefit: With each tour, Board Members will learn more and more.)

3) As you did as you followed up on the mailing from Strategy #8, let the conversation go towards brainstorming ideas together. You might toss out a problem the organization has had, to get your friend's ideas for possible solutions. Or the conversation may lead towards how she would love to get her kids' school involved. Or if your friend sits on the board of another nonprofit, you might share approaches your different organizations are taking re: the same issues. The important thing is that you bring it back to "Why them?" Perhaps you need assistance getting the word out to parents and teens who might use your counseling services. Perhaps you need volunteers to help move to a new, larger facility. By now, you and your friend will likely have all kinds of ideas, and she will likely have all kinds of input for you.

4) Here is the part for those who are bemoaning, "Our facility is just a bunch of offices!" Start the tour in one of those offices. Have the ED tell the story while sitting in that office - everything she would have told if this were a tour of grander facilities. Then, after telling the story of the work you do and the lives you affect, and after talking about some of the needs, tour the facility. It will not matter any more that it is just offices. "This is sometimes the only place a child feels safe and nurtured," your ED tells your friend. "It may look like just an office, but to some of the kids who get help here, this place represents caring. Sometimes it is their only hope..."

5) After the tour, the Board Member will follow up with a thank you note, whether or not the ED is going to do his/her own thank you note. You can never say thank you too many times.

Bringing people to your organization, and letting someone knowledgeable tell them the organization's story one-on-one, is a critical component to building relationships.

Make sure your new friend is added to the organization's mailing list. When the next newsletter goes out, add a personal note, reminding your friend of all he learned on the tour and of all you learned from his ideas. And for future mailings, remember to maintain that ongoing relationship, whether that is done by the Board Member, or by the staff or another volunteer.

SPECIAL NOTE: If your guest is a Board Member or volunteer from another organization, the next step may be a tour of *their* organization, so you can continue the dialogue and learn from them! For more about engaging with other nonprofit organizations, see Strategies #78-82.

What is the Role of the Board Member in this Strategy?

As a Board Member, it does not have to be your job to lead the tour - that can be left to someone who knows the organization well, usually the Executive Director or other key staff person. The Board Member's role in this activity is simply to invite his/her friends, make arrangements for the tour, and to join them during the tour.

AT THE DIAPER BANK

At the Diaper Bank, our first tour happened the year we collected 300,000 diapers. Because an office filled with diapers is not something you would see every day, we invited local dignitaries to come see the fruits of our labors. A local bank president, city council members, all our sponsors and even some prospective sponsors were "toured" through our 800 square foot office filled with diapers.

That was when we realized the power of having someone standing right beside us, as we tell the story of our mission.

When we finally had a warehouse for all those diapers, things changed. While an office full of diapers is silly, a warehouse full of diapers is - well - dull. Our mission is not warehousing, so do we really want to spend precious time showing folks the intricacies of our storage program? And in truth, even if our mission were just about diapers, we could do little more than point to those racks, saying, "Yup - there they are! Just look at them all!"

Hildy discussing issues with Congressman Jim Kolbe in the Diaper Bank warehouse

Instead, we would tell the stories. Stories of an African American baby who had been so chronically in the same diaper, his skin was permanently bleached in that shape. Stories of the elderly man who wept, thanking us for the supplies we gave him, as he had not been out of his home for 3 years, due to the fear of embarrassment and his inability to afford incontinence supplies. Stories of the very people who provide the Diaper Bank's warehousing functions - the developmentally disabled, some of whom cannot live independently without incontinence supplies.

Tours of the warehouse were suddenly an enlightening experience, primarily because the tour really was not about the diapers - it was about the issues at the core of the need for those diapers. Our goal became

encouraging people to ask the obvious questions - the ones we knew others were thinking: Why can't they just use cloth diapers? (Many day care centers do not accept cloth.) Don't the manufacturers donate diapers? (No.) We would strive to see how many times we could make someone say, "I never thought of that!"

Our tours became myth-busting sessions, awareness sessions about what life is really like when you are poor and trying to survive. Yes, we did those tours in the warehouse, but in truth, the same tour could have been done over lunch at someone's home - and often is.

A tour is only as good as the emotions it brings out in the people who attend. Our dull warehouse comes alive when we tell our stories. And that is all a tour needs to be.

Diaper Bank Board Member, giving a "tour" at the warehouse

Brainstorm Sheet: _____

❖ Meeting One on One

Personal Advocacy - Talking Points
What are the talking points every Board Member should be sharing as personal advocates for the organization?

1.) _____
2.) _____
3.) _____
4.) _____
5.) _____
6.) _____

Introductory Mailing
What topics should Board Members be looking for in the newspaper? What issues that have been discussed in the news are similar to the issues your organization is hoping to impact?

1.) _____
2.) _____
3.) _____
4.) _____
5.) _____
6.) _____

Breakfast with Friends
What are the three most important topics to be sure you share with your friend over breakfast?

1.) _____
2.) _____
3.) _____

Brainstorm Sheet: ▬▬▬▬ Sheet Two

❖ Meeting One on One

Community Sleuthing
As you read the sleuthing questions on page 49, what questions could you ask that are specifically related to your organization's mission and programs?

1.) _____

2.) _____

3.) _____

4.) _____

5.) _____

6.) _____

Hosting a Tour:
Have your Executive Director tour your board around the facility as if this were a "real" tour for new friends. What are the issues that jump out at you as she speaks? What are the hot buttons? Keep these in mind as you invite others to tour, perhaps creating a script from that "practice" tour.

_____

_____

_____

_____

_____

_____

Follow-Up Activities:
After you have connected your organization with your friend, how will the organization maintain that relationship?

3 months after the introduction _____

6 months after the introduction _____

1 year after the introduction _____

2 years after the introduction _____

❖ Introducing Whole Groups to the Organization via Informal Board Member Parties

Matchmaking does not have to be a one-on-one experience. A small comfortable gathering can also serve as a way to engage your friends with your organization's mission. In this section, you will find some ways to bring your organization's mission to groups of your friends, in a way that feels social, natural, and just plain fun.

The Board Member's role in these efforts is the primary role. These will be your own personal parties, with your own friends. While the organization's staff may be involved in some of these activities, the primary mover and shaker in these efforts is each individual Board Member.

Informal Board Member Parties

#12 - #14 Host an Event at Your Home

#15 - #20 Birthday Parties

Host an Event in Your Home

As my extended family of three teenagers entered high school, they quickly realized their education to date had not included learning to write essays. Suddenly they hit 9th grade and had assignments due and no clue where to start. In turn, each one came to me for tutoring.

Because most of their essays would be literary analyses ("Discuss the character development in Moby Dick," and etc.), I thought it might be easier for them to learn to write about movies.

So every Saturday for a month, we would watch a movie, and the kids would write a short essay afterward. I chose movies of a similar theme so they could compare and contrast - another favorite approach for high school essays.

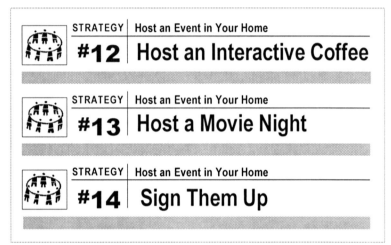

STRATEGY | Host an Event in Your Home
#12 | **Host an Interactive Coffee**

STRATEGY | Host an Event in Your Home
#13 | **Host a Movie Night**

STRATEGY | Host an Event in Your Home
#14 | **Sign Them Up**

For a reason I cannot recall, the theme I chose was prison movies.

We started with the 1932 black and white "I Am a Fugitive from a Chain Gang." We watched Burt Lancaster in "Birdman of Alcatraz" and Tim Robbins in "The Shawshank Redemption". We talked about the movies, and then the kids compared and contrasted. By the time they were done, they were thinking life in prison might just be better than having to watch another prison movie!

But something else happened in that month full of movies: the kids were changed by what they saw and the discussions that followed. They began to see those movies as a statement about our society rather than as pure entertainment. At the beginning of the month, they were writing about characters and plot. By the end of that month, their essays were about injustice and human cruelty.

When we experience a movie or presentation in the comfort and privacy of our homes, with our friends gathered around to discuss what we have seen together, it provides more than just an entertaining time. It allows real discussion of real issues. And that can make for a powerful effect. Just ask our kids!

What Are Events in My Home?

Sometimes introducing your friends to your organization requires little more than inviting friends to your home. As we have repeated often, these are not fundraising events. You will not be charging to attend the party, nor will your friends be strong-armed while they are there. The point of these events is fun, connection, mission, real engagement - not money.

And while movie parties are great fun and make for easy discussion of themes, there are other ways to introduce friends to the organization, in the comfort of your own home. We list a few here, but we know you will think of others.

What is the Goal of these Events?

Events in your home are intended to bring together the mission you care about and the friends you care about. The goal of each of the events will be to make that connection - to introduce your friends to the organization, with the hope that you will ignite the desire to become more deeply engaged with your organization's mission and vision.

Who Should We Invite?

The list is really up to you. You might invite just those friends you are closest to, or invite people you have wanted to see for a long time but never have time to catch up with. You could invite only those you think might be interested in your organization's work. Or you might invite everyone on your Life List. It is your home, and only you can decide who you want in your home!

How to Host an Event in Your Home

The following are just two approaches to hosting an event in your home. It is our hope these will spark other ideas - ideas more particular to your own tastes, the region you live in, local celebrations, and your organization's mission.

Note: If your community has been overwhelmed with a fundraising method that approaches the first event as a no-ask event, only to have the 2nd step be an invitation to a strong-armed ask for money, you might clarify that this is really and truly a no-ask event, with no strings attached - period.

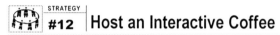

STRATEGY
#12 | **Host an Interactive Coffee**

An Interactive Coffee is an event where friends gather at your home for coffee (or wine and cheese, or brunch, etc.). This will *not* be a standard "coffee," with a talk by the Executive Director followed by passing the hat. This is *not* an arm-twisting event, as you will *not* be asking for money.

This will instead be an Interactive Coffee, where your guests will learn about your organization's mission by taking a few moments to immerse themselves in the issues your organization addresses.

First, have your Executive Director give a brief talk about the organization - less than 10 minutes. If your organization has a 5-7 minute video, you might substitute that for your ED's talk.

Then the fun begins - an audience participation piece to engage the group directly with your mission. That interactivity will link your guests' hearts to the critical importance of the work you do.

This interactive audience participation piece will vary depending on your mission. For example, if your mission is poverty-related, you might provide pencils and paper, and have the group try to budget their own monthly needs using a monthly income level that is just above the federal poverty line, making the task harder to accomplish, due to the lack of assistance programs.

Or if your mission is environmental, provide the various trade-offs your particular community is facing, using the same pencil-and-paper approach. Hand the problem to the group, and have them see how difficult the trade-offs are. Have them spend time considering the community they want to leave for their kids and their grandkids.

In each case, the question you ask will be similar: *Given these choices, what would you do?*

The same approach can be taken with any mission. All it takes is a bit of creativity to find a way to have your friends personally experience why your work is so important.

The benefit of an Interactive Coffee is the ability to engage with a small group, and to have them actively integrate your mission into their thinking by putting themselves in the shoes of those who are directly affected by your organization's work.

Another benefit is that the Coffee can be done in an hour, on your friends' way home from work. You may want to promise to stick to an hour, to give folks one more reason to fit this into their day.

STRATEGY #13 | Host a Movie Night

If you want to take the "coffee" approach one step further, host a movie night. Invite folks for a light supper (or make it a pot luck), and show a movie whose theme fits with the mission of your organization. *

For over 100 years, movies have been part of our world, which means virtually every topic under the sun has been covered in a movie - and probably a good movie at that! Mental health. Dance. Saving riparian areas. Music and theater and the power of the arts. Hunger. War. Cultural heritage.

As you did with the Interactive Coffee event, have your Executive Director present. He/she should be there from the start - mingling throughout dinner and enjoying the movie with the rest of the guests.

Then, after the movie, introduce your ED. Let your friends know, "Because the movie has so much to do with the work we do at XYZ Organization, I have asked our Executive Director to take a few minutes to talk more about this topic. Please feel free to ask her as many questions as you have!"

This will ***not*** be the 10 minute presentation your ED did during the coffee. After all, your guests have already sat for 2 hours to watch the movie! This talk should take just a few minutes to relate your mission to what they have seen in the movie, and to invite them to learn more. "Remember where the heroine _____? Well that happens all the time at our organization. And actually, the movie glossed over the reality of it. Just last week..." Have your Executive Director invite anyone who is interested in learning more to talk with her afterwards, or to arrange for a tour. And if your ED's talk goes longer than 5 minutes, get the hook and gently (or not so gently) let your guests go home while they are still excited about the work your organization is doing!

STRATEGY #14 | Sign Them Up!

For either of these events (or others you may come up with), have a sign-up sheet, listing various ways to further engage your guests. You might consider mixing things like "I'd like to take a tour" with some of the items on your organization's wish list. Keep the sign-up sheet on the food/beverage table, and throughout the evening, let your friends volunteer themselves. You might consider having one friend "seed" the list with his name, to encourage others to do the same.

Then, if a topic comes up in conversation, encourage your friends: "Would you put your name on the list for that?" They will.

As part of her presentation, your Executive Director might list one or two items from that list. "If you have a pick-up truck and can help us out during the week, we sure could use that!" Again, go gently if you choose to ask for things, and remember - this is not the time to ask for money. This is the time to build friendships and engage folks with your issues.

The following is an example of a sign-up sheet for this type of event. Modify it as makes sense for your organization. And if nothing else, get those names into your database, for sending your newsletter and other mailings as ongoing follow-up.

---

* For an off-the-top-of-the-head list of movies to start your creative juices flowing, turn to the AfterWords.

SAMPLE SIGN-UP SHEET

Contact Information	Volunteer	Provide In-Kind Assistance	I'd like to take a tour	Help Spread the Word	Other
Mary Rodriguez 5644 W. 10th Street 555-6868 Mary@10thSt.com	I can help with the upcoming event				
Susie Sigmund 1201 E. Spring St. 555-9043 Susie@SpringStreet.com		My business will help with printing!		X	
Ben Shapiro 4044 Olive Grove 555-2368 Ben@OliveGrove.com			X		My daughter needs to complete community service hours

What is the Role of the Board Member in this Strategy?

By now you guessed it - your role will be everything from doing the inviting to cleaning up afterwards.

AT THE DIAPER BANK

Back in 1992, when State funding for childcare was about to be cut by the Arizona legislature, the Diaper Bank realized the crippling effects that would have on a parent's ability to work.

Rather than just make a few phone calls, we chose to get the word out to a whole army, encouraging them to make those calls themselves. But we knew if we were to just send out an email or a form letter, it was likely our request would land in the trash.

So instead, we held Interactive Coffees in the homes of some of our supporters. And rather than doing a 10 minute pitch and then asking folks to fill out a postcard (standard coffee fare, ala political coffees), we proposed the following scenario:

> "Dad works at the industrial plant, making $12/hour. Mom is working retail part time and attends the community college for nursing. The kids are 4 and 2 - the baby still in diapers."

We showed how this working family made too much to qualify for assistance, and showed how the daycare cuts would not only stop mom from working, but would stop her from going to school to advance herself and her family.

We handed a pad and pencil to those in attendance and asked, "What would you do? How would you survive? What decisions would you have to make?" They learned in a flash what is meant by the words "Working Poor".

When they were done marveling at how families survive on these wages, we asked them to make calls, encouraging the legislature to assist families in their struggle to become self-sufficient.

Was this more powerful than sending out a postcard? And did the folks who attended those sessions become friends? The answer to both is, "You bet!"

Birthday Parties

The woman was barely 5 feet tall, but she stood straight and proud. "I turned 50 this weekend, and I told my friends not to bring gifts - to bring enough diapers to stack them taller than me," she told us. "And look!" she said. Package by package, she stacked them in our office. Then she stood next to them, far taller than she had been before she told us her story.

	STRATEGY	Birthday Parties
	#15	**Collection of Goods**
	STRATEGY	Birthday Parties
	#16	**Cash Donations**
	STRATEGY	Birthday Parties
	#17	**Party on Site**
	STRATEGY	Birthday Parties
	#18	**A Work Party**
	STRATEGY	Birthday Parties
	#19	**Thank You Notes**
	STRATEGY	Birthday Parties
	#20	**Create a How-to Fact Sheet**

What Do Birthday Parties Have to Do With Your Organization?

Any celebration that gathers people together is an occasion to introduce your friends to your organization. Birthday parties for the young and old, anniversary parties, retirement parties, holiday parties - any gathering is a great time to create a bigger celebration - a celebration of your organization and the community you serve.

What is the Goal of this Strategy?

There are so many ways to use parties to tie people to your organization, that the goals will vary as well. It is always fun and easy to brainstorm all kinds of ways to use parties to raise support for your cause. Looking at the goals in your organization's annual plans, you may find many of those goals can be furthered by these gatherings of friends.

Who Will We Include in this Strategy?

This strategy will apply to anyone having a birthday, anniversary, retirement or other party - including the people on your list who have children. And it will especially relate directly to you!

Strategies for Using Parties to Benefit Your Organization

Depending on the nature of your organization, the strategies for using parties to your advantage are limited only by your imagination. Here are just some - but we bet you will think of others!

 STRATEGY **#15** | Collection of Goods

Organizations of all types need "stuff." Crisis nurseries need baby supplies. The humane society needs dog food, leashes. Domestic violence shelters need women's hygiene supplies and school supplies for kids. Children's art programs need art supplies. Your organization likely has a wish-list published in every newsletter.

Parties create a great way to turn that wish list into a friend-connector. The process involves 2 steps.

1) Ask for Stuff
For an adult party of any kind (birthday, retirement, anniversary, etc.), a simple request on the invitation is all that is needed: "Because Jim is on the board of the homeless shelter, in lieu of gifts, please bring a blanket for the families the shelter helps."

For a child's birthday party, where the child will likely be *loudly* disappointed if all he gets is cans of food for the food bank, you might ask parents of the guests to bring a can of food in addition to their gift, to be donated in their child's name.

2) Tell the Story
The point of this effort is not the stuff your friends bring (although that is always helpful). The point is how you leverage that gift into the beginning of a real engagement between your friends and the work your organization does.

At the party, gather folks around and take 2 minutes to tell the story of the organization. "We cannot believe this pile of blankets! You all are amazing! And while we have you captive here, eating and drinking and celebrating, we wanted to take just a moment to tell you why the shelter has become so important to us..."

End your 2 minute pitch by telling your guests, "I don't want to take any more time away from your partying. But if you want to know more, please ask us. We love to talk about the shelter!"

 **STRATEGY #16 | Cash Donations**

We have all become so used to "raising friends so we can raise money." The point of this strategy is to turn that phrase around. In this activity, we will be asking for money as a path to raising friends!

First, include on the invitation the request that, in lieu of gifts, guests send a check to the organization in honor of your big day. Include an address for sending those donations, or you might consider including a form or donor envelope to facilitate that gift. (Use of the envelope will depend on the occasion and the relationships you have with your guests. What may be appropriate in some circumstances may be tacky in others.) Most people will send a token amount - $25 or so.

But remember - the fundraising potential is *not* why you are doing this! You are doing it so you can gather your friends around, to tell them why their gifts are so meaningful, just as Strategy #15 suggests above.

Again, this approach asks in a socially acceptable manner, and yet it provides you with a forum for a brief pitch. "Thank you all for being here - it means so much to me. A number of you have asked about the XYZ Group - the group we asked you to donate to in lieu of bringing a gift. I wanted to take a moment to tell you about why I care so much about this group...." You do not need to take any more than 2 minutes to thank your guests for their gifts, tell a story, and invite them to learn more.

STRATEGY #17 | Party on Site

This is a great approach for Board Members of arts and tourism and environmental groups - these and similar organizations are often drawn to this strategy. Depending on the nature of your organization, hosting parties at your facility can be a great way to engage new friends - young and old - in the mission work you do. (Remember: A party at the zoo is *not* just for kids!)

The party could be a tour, a performance, a reading, or some other active and hopefully interactive event. The botanical gardens may let young children plant their own plants or play with worms, while the tour for adults may focus on plants that bloom at night, or may simply be hosted at the facility, with a 5 minute talk by the Executive Director (or the Board Member who invited the guests). The same for the art museum, the theater group, the local historical society.

The obvious benefit from this type of party is direct engagement, for both kids and adults. This is a captive audience that can be told of the importance of your organization's work. Kids can be engaged to want to do more to help you. And at a different level, the same will be true for adults.

The more fun you make it, the more the attendees will want to come back to learn more, to participate on their own - or to have their own party!

STRATEGY #18 | A Work Party

As more and more people think of giving back as a way to celebrate the key moments of their lives, a Work Party may be a way for your organization to capitalize on this trend. While this type of effort is not an ongoing need for most organizations, there are indeed some organizations that require ongoing physical labor to support their work.

A good example of this type of effort might be working on a house for Habitat for Humanity. Helping with the ongoing manual labor needs of a local nature preserve is another example - and one that is often set in the most beautiful areas of your community. Helping serve dinner at the local soup kitchen is yet another example of a volunteer Work Party. Depending on the work your organization does, a work party might fit well with your mission.

These events can have multiple benefits. You will obviously get some great volunteers for the day. But you will also be exposing your organization's mission to new audiences in a way that will stick in the memories of young and old alike. And while you are working, you will have great opportunities to take folks on tours, talk about the issues - true engagement!

STRATEGY #19 | Thank You Notes

If your friends had brought you a personal gift, you would have sent them a thank you note. And that is just what you will do for the gifts they did bring - the cash or the "stuff" or the time they spent at your facility. In your note, let them know again what this means to you and to the organization. If the party you had was not at your organization's facility, offer to take them on a tour, or tap into something they had mentioned at the party. Use your thank you note as one more way to connect.

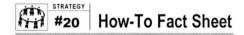
STRATEGY #20 | How-To Fact Sheet

There are often times when volunteers and others who are already friends of your organization will ask, "Is there anything more I can do?" By creating a How-To Fact Sheet, you can spread the party idea beyond just the immediate family of your board.

The How-To sheet should describe the options your organization suggests for these kinds of parties, from simply collecting goods or asking for "checks in lieu of gifts", to doing on-site parties or tours for kids of all ages, etc. Obviously these options will differ from organization to organization.

When individuals ask how they can help the organization, this is one of the many tools you can provide to them - something that is easy, and yet helpful in so many ways. And it is a great way to extend your FriendRaising campaign, as *they* bring *their* friends into the fold!

What is the Role of the Board Member in this Strategy?

The first and easiest role for Board Members is to use one or more of these strategies for their own parties. Then, to the extent possible without creating the family equivalent of an international incident, use these approaches for parties of family members - spouses, children, etc.

Lastly, Board Members should send the "How-To" sheet to those friends they feel comfortable approaching, perhaps some of the people on their Life Lists. Parents of school-aged children should especially be encouraged to consider your organization for some kind of party, as more and more parents wonder how to teach their kids about giving back (and wonder how to out-do their child's last birthday party!)

AT THE DIAPER BANK

The Diaper Bank has been the beneficiary of so many parties it is overwhelming. The mom who asked everyone who attended her 4 year old's birthday party to please remember those not as fortunate as her son, and bring a package of diapers. The golf buddies of a 65 year old who celebrated her birthday with a card filled with checks to the Diaper Bank. A supporter who has a holiday pot luck every year at her home, with admittance being one tasty dish and a package of diapers.

For Dimitri's 50th birthday, we had a picnic in the park and asked everyone to please bring a package of adult incontinence supplies. At least this way the gag gifts would have some use beyond making money for the novelty shop!

The Diaper Bank may not have a beautiful facility where a birthday party would be elegant and fun - the zoo, the botanical garden, the art museum. But we have learned there is always a way to have such a celebration honor the work the Diaper Bank does.

Brainstorm Sheet:

Sheet One

❖ Informal Board Member Parties

Interactive Activities for Coffees

Brainstorm interactive activities that take about 10-15 minutes, that could show a group the essence of your mission. Don't limit your thinking to only "sedate" ideas - get crazy and creative, and then narrow down the options. Some of the sanest programs come from the most "out there" initial ideas!

If it helps spark your thinking, consider the question you want the group to answer, and work your way backwards to determine how you might get to that question. For example, if the question is, "What would you do?", what scenarios might lead up to that question as it relates to your mission?

_____

_____

_____

_____

_____

_____

_____

What movies relate to the mission of your organization?
(See the AfterWords for some thought-starters.)

_____

_____

_____

_____

_____

_____

_____

Brainstorm Sheet: ━━━━━━ Sheet Two

❖ **Informal Board Member Parties**

Create a How-To Sheet for Birthday Parties

Using the ideas in this section, as well as other ideas you come up with, create an idea list for how birthday parties can help your organization. What kinds of parties could those be? What are your needs, that guests might provide? When the list is completed, put it on letterhead and share it with friends.

Note:

While this fact sheet could be created by staff and simply provided to Board Members to distribute, this activity is far too much fun to leave Board Members out of the brainstorming process. And besides, it will be your Board Members' birthdays you will be celebrating!

_____

_____

_____

_____

_____

_____

_____

Follow-Up Activities:

After you have connected your organization with your friends, how will the organization maintain those relationships?

3 months after the introduction   _____

6 months after the introduction   _____

1 year after the introduction   _____

2 years after the introduction   _____

❖ Introducing Whole Groups to the Organization via Organized On-Site Events

The previous section focused on informal parties, created by Board Members around their own private celebrations. This section focuses on events that are organized by the whole board (or the whole organization).

The intent of these events is engagement, just as it was in the prior section. The difference is that these events are focused on the work your organization does - the nuts and bolts of what it takes to make your mission happen. Whether getting their hands dirty at a volunteer event, getting their minds wrapped around a particular issue at a focus-group event, or celebrating the organization's successes and plans at an Annual Meeting Event, these events all engage your friends directly in the mission work your organization is about at its core.

Camaraderie and synergy are the keys to this section, where introductions to new friends happen as part of a larger group activity. Whether they are sharing their wisdom, their labor, or their celebration, your friends will be invited to join something big and blossoming - the relationships you are building with the whole community.

The Board Member's role in these efforts will vary depending on the event. The common theme will be "ambassador" - the diplomat who represents the organization in a gracious manner, hosting friends as the honored guests they are.

Strategies for Organized On-Site Events

#21 - #23 Barn Raising (a.k.a. Volunteer Parties)

#24 Focus Group Event

#25 - #26 Annual Meeting Event

Barn Raising (a.k.a. Volunteer Parties)

Nothing builds friendships faster than working side by side. We learned that in 1998, when the 300,000 diapers we collected all wound up in our tiny consulting office. The "barn-raising" event that rid our offices of those diapers has become such a cornerstone of the Diaper Bank's year that donors, dignitaries and our most avid supporters have been known to ask, "When is

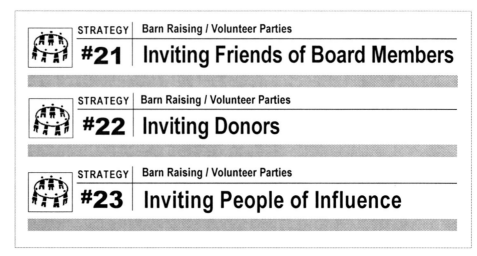

	STRATEGY	Barn Raising / Volunteer Parties
	#21	**Inviting Friends of Board Members**
	STRATEGY	Barn Raising / Volunteer Parties
	#22	**Inviting Donors**
	STRATEGY	Barn Raising / Volunteer Parties
	#23	**Inviting People of Influence**

the next diaper hurl?" Yes, once a year you can find City Council members, major philanthropists and local celebrities hurling and sorting and schlepping diapers, getting sweaty and dirty in the process and having a terrific time.

What is a Barn-Raising / Volunteer Party?

If you have ever seen the 1960's musical "Seven Brides for Seven Brothers," you have seen the classic example of a Volunteer Party - the barn raising. In the days of the American frontier, when someone needed to build a barn, neighbors would gather to make that chore go far more quickly than any one family could do on its own. What might otherwise take weeks to complete could be done in a day.

Perhaps the modern-day equivalent of a barn-raising would be having friends over to paint your house, or to help you move. When a task is turned into a social event, it is no longer work. It becomes instead the best kind of party - the kind where folks naturally get to know each other, without any pressure.

In creating your Volunteer Party, your thinking will change from

> *"We have a huge project to do. We always have such trouble getting volunteers. Maybe a scout troop will help, or a seniors group..."*

>> to

> *"We have a huge project to do. This will be a great opportunity to bring 50 people to our organization who do not know much about us, and to introduce them to our mission! While we work, we can mingle and talk with them one by one about why the work they are doing is so important. It will be personal, and those individuals will be buying into our mission with their own hands!"*

While this type of event works well for any volunteer need, if the task requires manual labor, that is when the real fun begins. Grown-ups do not typically have the opportunity to gather with other grown-ups and get dirty and sweaty, especially in a setting where it is all for a good cause. And like the barn-raising in days of old, nothing builds bonds faster than a group of people all pitching in together.

So if you are moving your office to a bigger location, **have a party!**
If the grounds around your facility are looking a bit shabby, **have a party!**
If it is time for your annual mailing, **have a party!**

What is the Goal of This Effort?

The goal of volunteer parties is not just to get the work done. As a matter of fact, we have created volunteer parties when the work to be done probably could have been accomplished by a handful of people in just a few hours.

The real purpose of these parties is to introduce people to your organization in a highly personal yet disarming way. These may be individuals who know nothing of your cause, or who may have written checks but never been part of the fabric of what you do.

The goal for those who actually attend and help out is to have them physically participate in the work your organization does. That gives you the opportunity to talk with them personally about why that work is important, while they are physically connecting to that work. This double-whammy will reinforce their support for the work you do, creating a deep engagement from the very start.

There is equal importance, though, for the people who cannot attend the event. Done well, you will be connecting with these individuals in a personal, nonthreatening way that is not asking them for anything. In other words, you will be opening a dialogue, a relationship - all based on their receiving an invitation.

Who Should We Invite?

Because at least part of the reason for this party is to actually get real work done, before you begin creating your invitation list, the first step will be to determine how many people are needed to accomplish the task at hand. That will be the basis for estimating the number of attendees / invitees.

To estimate that number, use the following formula:

> 1) Determine how many volunteers you think will be required to complete the task
>
> 2) Now double that number. Or if you have a lot of space, triple it.

Why double or triple the number? Because the purpose of the party is not just to get work done, but to also add X new people to your list of friends. So figure out if you can do more work, or do it differently, if you have more people on hand. And that inflated number of volunteers will be the number of people you will want to have attend.

Note: Do not count Board Members among the workers. Board Members will have a special job during this event, but it will <u>not</u> be to get a lot of work done.

Divide the number of attendees by the number of people on your board, and the result will be the number of friends each Board Member will be responsible for bringing to the event. Give each Board Member invitations, and have them report their list of invitees to the coordinator of this event (probably a staff person, but not necessarily), to ensure there are no duplicates among Board Members.

 STRATEGY #21 | **Inviting Friends of Board Members**

> Board Members should review their Life Lists to see who they would like to invite, because in truth, anyone on your Life List could be a candidate for inviting to this event. If there is something in particular that makes you consider one or more specific individuals at this time, invite whomever makes the most sense. Because a volunteer event is one of the most disarming ways to introduce your personal friends to your organization's work, you may find you want to invite your whole list.

STRATEGY #22 | **Inviting Donors**

In our experience it is the rare organization that thinks of its donors as volunteers, as real friends. Because they already give money, we do not often involve them in much of anything else. And that is truly a missed opportunity, for both your organization and your donors.

While we may nurture relationships with some of our largest donors, when it comes to those who give smaller amounts, the reality is we often take them for granted. We do not know many of those smaller donors personally, and aside from perhaps an annual donor recognition event or holiday open house, we do not typically invite our smaller donors to participate in anything they do not have to pay to attend.

But that was before we stopped thinking of them as "donors" and started thinking of them as "friends." When we start seeing our "donors" as real "friends," and we start seeing a "party" instead of just "finding some volunteers and getting the job done," all kinds of magic happens. That is because you would not think of having a party without inviting the friends who show you repeatedly throughout the year how much they care about you - and that is just what those friends are doing when they send $25 or $100 every few months!

By sending all your donors an invitation to experience hands-on the work they are already supporting with their dollars, you are inviting them to become real friends. Depending on the event, you will be surprised how many of your donors - from your $25 donors up to your largest donors - will RSVP to come to join in the fun.

AT THE DIAPER BANK

In Phoenix, the first Diaper Drive happened before there was much of an organization in place to handle the results. A Volunteer Party was the only way to get 100,000 diapers sorted and distributed quickly!

When we showed up to help that day, we asked the folks working beside us, "How did you hear about today's event?" They told us they had sent a $25 check after reading about the Diaper Drive in the newspaper, and they could not have been more excited to have been invited to help with their hands as well as their purses. "No one has ever asked us to help like this before. It is such fun! We can't wait to do more."

Donors can be more than donors - they can be friends, if only we would ask them!

 STRATEGY #23 | **Inviting People of Influence**

While this might better fit in the next section on "Making New Friends," if you are already creating a Matchmaking event to introduce Board Members' existing friends to the organization, why not also see if you can meet some folks you do not already know, but would love to know!

List the 10 or 20 or 50 people in your community you would love to be able to show more about your organization. It could be the Mayor, or local business leaders, or local philanthropists. Send them *all* invitations, regardless of how many people you think you might need to do the work. The reason for that is simple - most of these people will not show up. But their showing up is not the point.

The point is to give you a good reason to get in touch with them, to introduce your organization without asking for anything but to share a good time.

Divide those names among Board Members, and have Board Members call to confirm the invitation was received, and to see if that person might attend. Chances are they will not be able to participate, but now you will have made initial contact with the 50 people you most want to know! And as you will see in the following pages, this introduction will be followed up, again in a non-threatening, engaging way.

How to Do a Volunteer Party

The main thing to remember about your volunteer party is that it is just that - a party! And just like any other party, you will invite people in a way that is inviting! Then, once your guests arrive, you will make them feel welcome and make sure they have fun. And afterwards, you will follow up, thanking them for being part of your special day.

Create Invitations

The first step is to create party invitations. This will not be a call for volunteers, asking for help with your mailing (as an example). Instead, you will create real invitations:

It's a Newsletter Mailing Party!
Pizza and Sodas and Tons of Fun!
Bring the kids and show them how to help give back!

You get the idea. You can print these invitations on your computer - it does not have to be fancy. The point is that people know they will have fun and help out at the same time.

On the Day of the Event

- Have a sign-in sheet for guests to provide name / address / phone / company or affiliation / email address / etc. You will not be able to send them a thank you or put them on your mailing list if you do not have this information.

- Have everyone wear name tags. Guests should be able to easily get to know each other.

- Have music. Have snacks or pizza. Remember - it's a party!

- *Critical for Success:* Before you get the work started, gather folks around and have the ED spend no more than 3 minutes talking not about "what has to get done", but why you are all there in the first place. He/She should talk about the impact the organization has on the lives of real people, and then talk about how the work being done at today's party will have a direct impact on the people / animals / environmental areas / etc. your organization serves. Again, aim at a 3 minute maximum for this talk, to create the context for the day's work.

- *Critical for Success:* As the guests are working, the job of Board Members will be to shmooze, talk about the organization, answer questions, perhaps take one or two people on a tour - and yes, work with them side by side for a bit. But the main job of Board Members at this event will not be as a volunteer. It will be as an ambassador for the organization's mission. The job of Board Members will be to make friends.

- *Critical for Success:* Take a group photo. Do not let too many stragglers start to leave before gathering everyone for that photo. And the sweatier and messier they are, the better!

After the Event

There is no time more critical to the success of this event than the time period immediately after the event is over. As with most things in life, a bit of follow-up can make a huge difference.

This is where the photos come in. Print enough copies of the group photo for one to be sent to everyone who attended AND to those people who were not able to attend.

For Attendees:

- Board Members will write Thank You's to the people they invited, telling them not only how much their assistance was appreciated, but how much you enjoyed having the opportunity to tell them about the organization. If there was something in particular that sparked the guest's interest as you talked during the party, remind them of that in your note.

- Include a copy of the photo as a memento of the day. Regardless of how much people think they hate to have their picture taken, or how disheveled they may have been when the photo was taken, they love to get photo reminders of a fun time. They may throw out your newsletter, but the photo they will keep forever.

- Be sure to also make follow-up assignments for those who attended, but who were not specifically invited by a board member - donors, guests of other guests, etc. Make sure none of your new friends falls through the cracks!

- Add each individual to the organization's database, noting which Board Member brought that person in the door, to facilitate future follow-up.

For People Who Did Not Attend:

Board Member Invitees:

- Board Members will send notes to their own personal invitees who could not / did not show up. Include a copy of the photo, with a sticky-note that says, "This was such a fun morning. We hope you can join us next time!" This extends the relationship, and makes it logical when you make that call for your next event.

Dignitaries:

- Board Members will also send notes to the dignitaries they invited. As with Board Member invitees, include a copy of the photo, with a sticky-note that tells them that you hope they can join you next time.

- If you spoke with the person directly when you called prior to the event, make sure your note thanks them for taking a moment to speak with you. Offer to let them know more about the organization if they are interested.

For Everyone:

When it is time for your next newsletter, include a short article about the party, along with the photo, to get folks excited to attend next time!

> ### AT THE DIAPER BANK
>
> As part of our client work at Help 4 NonProfits, we were working with a local arts and education organization, where a number of the employees also happened to be Diaper Bank volunteers. When we were suggesting some community engagement approaches the client might consider, one of those volunteers said, "You know when we are going to start sorting diapers, and you talk to us about the fact that it's not about diapers, but about poverty and humanity? That is what we need to be doing when our volunteers show up!"

What is the Role of the Board Member in this Strategy?

While the staff may be the ones organizing this event and may be in charge of the logistics of the day's work, Board Members will be involved in this activity from start to finish. They will provide names of friends to invite; they will personally send those invitations (preferably with a personal note on each one); and they will follow up to see which of their friends will be attending. They will call to follow up with dignitaries. On the day of the party, they will mingle, tell stories of the organization, join staff members for tours. After the event, they will write notes to dignitaries and other friends who did not attend, urging them to participate next time. And of course, they will write thank you's to those who did show up and helped make the day a success.

THE DIAPER HURL

There are so many diapers in our office

WE ARE READY TO HURL!

The Diaper Bank has learned to turn everything into a party. When it is time to do the mailing for our annual appeal, we serve pizza and invite everyone from our local congressman to our donors. (A discussion with our Congressman over folding and stuffing led to Dimitri and me visiting with all the members of the Arizona Congressional Delegation in Washington, D.C., to talk about poverty and diapers!)

But the event most people wait for and love is our Annual Hurling Party.

In 1998, our 5th Annual December Diaper Drive collected almost twice what we had ever collected before - over 300,000 diapers. The diapers had arrived via individual donors carrying their individual packages up the stairs to our 2nd story walk-up office. Package by package, the diapers slowly piled up. Eventually they overran our tiny office.

So how do you get 300,000 diapers out of the office and delivered to the recipient agencies? The thought of marching each of those packages back out of our office and down the stairs was unbearable.

Sitting shoulder-deep in diapers as we considered our options, giddiness set in. "Can't we just toss these things over the balcony and be done with them?" we asked ourselves. I remember telling a friend on the phone, "We've got so many diapers in here, I am ready to hurl."

And down to the words, that is just what we did. The invitations read **"We've got so many diapers, we are ready to hurl!"**

The morning of the Hurling Party, a volunteer crew from Tucson Electric Power backed TEP's huge flatbed trucks underneath our balcony. Joining those volunteers were radio personalities, City Council members, donors, family and friends, who stationed themselves on the backs of those trucks, while another crew was positioned upstairs.

Before we began working, I gave a short talk that has become a tradition at all Diaper Bank Volunteer Parties. "While we are here today to hurl diapers," I started, "I want to remind you all that this is not about diapers. This is about people who cannot help themselves - the disabled, the elderly, and of course babies. This is about poverty and vulnerability, and the need for us to do far more than just help with their diapers. As you handle these thousands of diapers today, please take a moment to think about why you are doing this, why we are all doing this."

Then, with news cameras on hand to document the scene, we bucket-brigaded the diapers out of our office and towards the balcony. And we hurled those diapers into the waiting hands of the crews on the trucks.

Within just an hour and a half, all 300,000 diapers were off to the agencies who would provide them to clients. And a beloved annual event was born!

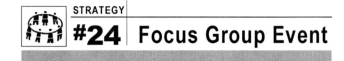

What is a Focus Group Event?

In the world of marketing, a focus group is a small sample group that is assembled to help determine how the population at large (or the targeted market for the product) would respond to various aspects of a product or issue. Do middle class women prefer this movie ending or another? Would teenaged boys use this product, or think it is beneath them? By assembling small representative groups of the target audience for a product, the folks in marketing hope to test their ideas about what products will sell, and how they should sell them.

Your organization will use focus groups to get fresh ideas about how to create more effective programs, and to get input about how to better engage with all facets of the community - from the people who could benefit from your program, to potential supporters, and everyone in between.

What Will Be the Goal of These Events?

For your organization, a Focus Group Event can be a great way to accomplish many things at once - another opportunity for deep engagement.

★ **The Opportunity to Learn and Enhance Your Programs:** The Focus Group Event allows you to receive feedback and outside perspectives on the work you are doing. These perspectives are one way to ensure your programs are well-rounded, as they will provide thoughts you might not otherwise have considered.

★ **The Opportunity to Spread the Word About Your Mission:** The Focus Group Event generates deeper knowledge of your programs and goals among the attendees

★ **The Opportunity to Engage Directly with Your Work:** By assisting you with making your programs better, the participants in your Focus Group Events will have commitment and buy-in to the work you are trying to do, creating a whole new group of deeply engaged friends.

The key is that one-two punch: The folks who attend become acquainted with and feel a bond with your programs, as they will have had input into how those programs operate. And at the same time, you will be gaining valuable insights into doing your job better. The Focus Group Event is really "Group Community Sleuthing."

Who Should We Invite?

This strategy will apply to the same people you listed for Community Sleuthing, and then some.

- Elected officials
- Individuals who seem to know everyone
- People who have led an interesting life
- Participants in your programs
- People who work at, or sit on the boards of organizations that do similar work to your organization

In addition, don't forget to invite those people in your community you would simply love to get to know.

How to Do a Focus Group Event

Focus Group Events are structured sessions with 10-15 people from all walks of life. The thing these individuals will have in common is an affinity for the work your organization does - whether as a donor, a vendor, a participant in the program, a friend of a Board Member, etc. The event takes no more than an hour - a nice thing to be able to promise people with otherwise busy lives. And out of courtesy to your guests, you will stick to that one-hour deadline, without exception.

The important thing to remember is that this is an event - a happening. It is not a "meeting" and it is not a "committee" - 2 words that cause the most energetic among us to glaze over. This is an event.

1) Send invitations. You can design those invitations on your computer, and you can buy blank invitation stock at your local office supply dealer for under $10 for a box of 50.

   The invitation should make clear that this event is not open to just anyone. You are inviting a small group of individuals whose specific expertise and "take" on the world you value. You want *their* specific knowledge, wisdom, and observations, even though they may not think they have anything special (most of us do not think we know half as much as we know!). The invitation should clearly state, "If you cannot attend, please do *not* send a substitute. We want *your* presence, *your* knowledge, *your* input."

2) During the event, the Event Leader (Executive Director, Board Member, knowledgeable staff person, etc.) will provide a BRIEF (+10 minutes) background about the organization, or a particular program you are about to launch. After that brief presentation, the leader will ask some of the questions in the box to the right (or create your own questions). Then he/she will invite discussion.

3) As it is with Community Sleuthing, now is the time to just be quiet, listen to the responses and the discussion, and take notes as each person expresses his/her views about the issues that are so close to your heart. It may sound corny, but truly the hardest part of these events is making sure your organization's representatives sit quietly and listen. It is hard to not participate, and it is harder still to stop yourself from jumping at the chance to say, "But we already do that!"

Questions for the Focus Group

Aim questions at building on the positive. What strengths should we emphasize? What community resources have we overlooked? How can we make it even better? Here are some examples:

- We want this program to help improve the quality of life in our community. Do you have thoughts on how we could maximize the impact the program has?

- What community assets and resources are you aware of, that we might tap into to maximize our effectiveness?

- As we publicize this program in the community, what parts of the program would you emphasize? Which part of what we are doing do you most identify with? Which parts excite you? How can we talk about those issues in a way that community members will identify with?

- (For human service providers) If a family member needed to use a service like ours, what questions would you want to know as you decided if our program was right for you? (For arts / education providers) If a family member were interested in the kind of work we are doing, what questions would you have before encouraging him/her to participate in this program? (Etc. for the specific discipline covered by your organization.)

Notice that these questions are about making the program the most effective it can be. The value will come from having great input for your program, and from the "ownership" each of these individuals will feel in your success.

To avoid the questions noted in the "Caution," prepare questions ahead of time and distribute them in writing. And make sure the Event Leader keeps the conversation on track.

The key in these sessions is to listen more than you talk, and to ask more than you answer. You have gathered these individuals in order to learn, not to persuade! Keeping quiet is the hardest part of doing this well.

4) Provide a "Keeping in Touch" sheet, asking for contact information, and also asking them to provide the names of 2 other people they think might be interested in helping you in this same manner - attending a similar event. Then use those names for the invitation list for your next Focus Group Event!

5) At the end of the session, ask each attendee for permission to call upon them again if you have other questions, especially after you have further considered the information they have provided to you. (Getting permission to call again gives you instant feedback.)

6) Stick to an hour. Out of respect for the time these busy people have given you, do not let the event go one minute past that hour. However, offer to tour the facility with anyone who is interested in lingering.

7) Follow up with a thank you note. If they have not already toured the facility, invite them to do so. (They may be too busy for a tour, but ask - you never know. Your Focus Group Event may have sparked their curiosity!).

8) Enter all attendees into your database, and make sure their contact information includes notes about their thoughts from the event. When mailings are sent to anyone who has attended a Focus Group Event, make sure it includes a special personal note, perhaps relating to thoughts they shared that day.

Having the focus group attendees engage themselves with the content of the program will turn participants into supporters of the program, as they will have had a hand in bringing it to fruition. Just as importantly, though, you will have the opinions of 10-15 smart people per group, providing insights about issues you may not have considered. The combination of those two benefits is what community engagement is all about.

CAUTION: Do NOT Ask These Questions

While you may be inclined to ask one of the following questions, please note that these are the *worst* questions you can ask:

- **"How can we raise money for this program?"**
- **"How can we raise awareness of this program?"**

Why are they the worst? Because the responses will be generic "tossing ideas against the wall" responses - an event here, a PSA there. And while that is always a lively conversation, it is *not* what you want. What you *do* want is for folks to engage seriously with ***the issues*** your organization is about, so they will not only provide you with substantive assistance regarding those issues, but will simultaneously engage themselves with the actual work you are doing.

If you find the group roaming into generic idea-tossing about marketing or fundraising, use your written questions to gently bring the group back where you want them - on the issues of your mission.

Make This an Ongoing Effort

If your Focus Group Event is as successful in generating real interest about your programs as those we have coordinated and participated in, you will want to do this event on an ongoing basis - perhaps monthly. There is always something new to ask, something new to learn, some new program or approach to explore, some new community issue to tackle. And you will find people remember these events for years, asking how a program is going, thinking about the issues long after the event.

By bringing a constant stream of people in to help you build upon your existing programs and create new ones, the organization creates that engaged energy each time, for each program.

What is the Role of the Board Member in this Strategy?

There are a variety of roles a board member can take in this effort.

- At minimum, every Board Member should invite people from his/her lists to these events, until all their contacts have either attended or gracefully bowed out of attending.

- Board Members who are so inclined can help "host" one of these events - simply providing the munchies, or the conference room space if it occurs off-site, and welcoming guests as they arrive.

- And finally, Board Members with extensive knowledge of the organization might choose to present the information and run the event as an Event Leader.

AT THE DIAPER BANK

The Diaper Bank's first focus group event was not intended as a means of getting the word out, but almost the complete opposite. We were in the process of creating a new program - an effort to raise awareness of what it is like to live in poverty. And we really wanted feedback. We had been developing the program ourselves, and we have been around long enough to know that when creative people breathe their own air for too long, the results might make sense to them, but may fall flat with a real audience. We needed someone to test this new program on!

We gathered a group of friends and supporters, and we asked them to be our guinea pigs. "Let us know what works / doesn't work about what we are planning to do. What parts are effective? Which parts are confusing? Which parts excite you, spark your curiosity?" We asked the normal questions one would ask when testing something new.

But here is what we had not counted on: We were not only getting their input and critique on our new program, but by doing so, we were exposing this group to the program itself. In the process we saw not only how effective the program would be when we produced it, but how effective the very act of testing it had been!

A new means for providing information was born. "How Are We Doing?" sessions became a great way of sharing our mission. And from those sessions, each individual came away saying, "I'd like you to do this presentation for our Rotary." "I'd like you to present this program for my book club." "I'd like this program to be the annual meeting topic for my women's group."

Annual Meeting Event

Mention the Annual Meeting, and most Board Members' eyes glaze over. Where they see tedium, though, we have seen opportunity for all kinds of connections with the community you serve.

	STRATEGY	Annual Meeting Event
	#25	**Annual Meeting Event**

	STRATEGY	Annual Meeting Event
	#26	**Photo "Thank You's"**

What is an Annual Meeting Event?

Most organizations' bylaws call for an annual meeting. This may be the time of year when officers are elected to the board, or when new Board Members rotate on while Board Members whose terms have expired rotate off. It may be when the Executive Director provides a "State of the Organization" address, or when the audit is presented. Many organizations simply take 20 extra minutes prior to or after their regular monthly business meeting, to accomplish these annual jobs, turning the annual meeting into more of a housekeeping task.

But imagine instead a celebration - an event that rejoices in all the accomplishments of the past year, while announcing the organization's goals for the coming year. An event that thanks donors and volunteers, and acknowledges the staff. An event that perhaps includes a tour, or perhaps a meal. An event that absolutely includes an exchange of goodwill, engaging those who have helped make the year a good one, and will help make next year an even better one.

What is the Goal of the Annual Meeting Event?

This will be the time of year when the organization shines, telling its story and announcing its plans for the year ahead. The goal of the annual meeting event is therefore to show the world how much your organization accomplishes and how grand its goals are, in a way that engages attendees to want to help turn those goals into reality. Ideally, you will create an event your guests will want to be invited to next year!

Who to Invite?

This is the time to invite everyone on your Life List. It is also the time to invite all the staff, all the donors, all the volunteers, all the past Board Members - anyone who is associated with the organization's success. And it is a great time to invite local dignitaries - both those who know you, and those you wish knew you better. You may even ask one or two of them to say a few words at the event.

If your organization is a human service organization, perhaps former clients could be there to talk about the importance of the organization. If your organization is a school, former students could do the same. If your organization is an advocacy group, perhaps legislators and city council members should be there - both current supporters and those you hope to woo.

And if you are going to tout achievements and future plans, don't forget to invite the press!

How to Use Your Annual Meeting as a Celebration

Your organization's annual meeting should be your organization's finest moment all year. And the ways of accomplishing that are as limitless as your imagination.

	STRATEGY	
	#25	**Creating an Annual Meeting Event**

The important thing as you consider this event is that you not only perform the necessary business as set out in your bylaws, but that you take time once a year to truly celebrate all you have accomplished, and to announce to the world what amazing adventures lie ahead.

So make it a party! Run tours of the facility, or have the Mayor say a few words. Cut the ribbon on a new wing. If yours is an arts group, show off your talents! Be creative and have fun. This is your day to shine!

Regardless of the format you choose, the focus of the event should be to highlight your accomplishments over the past year, to announce the organization's plans for impacting the community's quality of life in the coming year, and to invite your friends to link arms with you, heading into the upcoming year's adventures together.

Both before and after the presentation, the main job of everyone on staff and the whole board will be to "work the crowd" - to be the hosts of the party. The goal for each Board Member and staff person should be to proudly tell the story to as many individuals or groups of individuals as you can speak with and/or tour around; in other words, making friends. Depending on the size of the facility, organized group tours might be in order. But staff and Board Members should also be providing tours on an individual basis.

And as to the business meeting your board must hold to comply with your legal obligations, you can either hold that publicly or privately, depending on the nature of the meeting and depending on your bylaws.

 STRATEGY
#26 | Photo Thank You's as Another Point of Engagement

One of the easiest ways to have people remember your event fondly is to send a photo of them in attendance. Have at least one volunteer who is handy with a camera take digital photos of attendees having fun. You can pose groups of friends, or pose a Board Member and ED with a local dignitary, or just take candid shots of people enjoying themselves.

If you know someone who is knowledgeable in digital photography, printing the photo in a digitized "frame," with the organization's logo and the date of the event can turn each photo into something even more memorable. (If you do not have a volunteer or staff person who can do this, check with a local graphics firm or the graphics department at your local community college. The goodwill the photos provide is well worth the small expense of creating that frame and doing this part well.)

Send a personalized "thank you" note to everyone in attendance (have them sign in to ensure you capture their names and addresses), and include with that "thank you" note the photo of them enjoying your event.

Tucson's needy babies, elderly and disabled thank you! Diaper Sorting Party July 19, 2003

Southern Arizona Community Diaper Bank www.DiaperBank.org

Then add those individuals to your mailing list, and make sure each person who attended gets a personal note on each of their mailings from now on. For example, a handwritten note on your next newsletter might say, "After hearing about our plans for the year, I thought you might want to see how we are doing!" That is just one more step in maintaining the relationship with someone who cares.

Extra Tip
Send copies of the best of the photos to the society pages of your local newspaper, as well as using them for your newsletter.

What is the Role of the Board Member in this Strategy?

This strategy will rely as much upon the board as it does the staff - after all, this is the board's annual meeting! The board should be involved in planning the event, as well as executing the event. This could be done by a committee of the board, to include key staff members as well. It is also an excellent role for former Board Members, keeping them involved with the mission after their official post has expired.

Board Members will invite guests and act as hosts on the day of the event. Board Members will be involved in sending personal thank you notes to their guests, and most importantly, in following up with any interest shown in the organization by the guests in attendance.

Dinner and Awareness

Family Service is an organization in Lancaster, Pennsylvania, that provides services to support and strengthen families. Their last annual meeting was a typical dinner-with-speaker. But the topic was anything but typical.

According to Russ Burke, Family Service's VP for Development, after dinner, the staff provided information about a program that is, in Russ's words, "not warm and fuzzy" - their Batterers Intervention Service. They then visually showed their results:

"A large jar had been filled to the brim with wafers, 1/4 of them green, and the rest brown. The total wafers in the jar represented the number of domestic violence cases adjudicated in Lancaster County last year, while the green wafers represented the men that we treated…with excellent outcomes! The program director talked about the challenges of treating a sometimes distrustful and hostile population, and she talked about our successes."

Family Service made a bold choice, focusing the evening *not* on their more traditional "warm-and-fuzzy" programs, but on an issue that provokes and makes people think about things they might prefer not to think about. As a result, by the end of the evening, Family Service had not only made some great new friends, but they had reaffirmed the decision to join the board for one brand new board member, and recruited another!

Meeting and Conference in One

Amnesty International's annual meeting is held concurrently with its annual conference. The 2005 conference, for example, combined the following types of activities into 3 very full days:

- Member-only work, such as a board candidate forum, work sessions and discussion panels on policy resolutions, and actual resolution voting sessions

- For members and non-members alike, educational panels and workshops on a variety of topics related to Amnesty's work to end human rights abuses.

Make it 100% About the Mission

In the final analysis, it is not the size of the organization, the size of the community, or the celebrities you know that matter - it is the mission that matters the most, and the way you connect your organization with the community that will receive the benefit your organization provides.

In Blooming Prairie, Minnesota (population: 2,000), the Blooming Prairie Center has operated its youth-related services on a total budget of less than $100,000.

The organization was facing tough times when its new Executive Director, Katherine Driskell, was hired. The Center was losing money and in danger of closing, with its reputation in this small community fading fast. Therefore, according to Kathie, the goals for the Center's annual meeting were as follows:
  1) Comply with by-law requirements for the meeting
  2) Begin to restore the organization's stature and esteem in the community

The Center's teenage volunteers offered to host a taco night, to get as many people from the community as possible into the building to see the good things that were happening there. The format was informal - an open house with a few speakers, but mostly the kids and the Center's board members showing the community around the Center and talking to them about the Center's plans.

On the day of the event, 200 people showed up - 10% of the population of the whole town!

According to Kathie:
  "The teens put together posters highlighting theirs and the Center's accomplishments. As we all mingled with the crowd, we heard from folks who were part of our work way back when, some of the older men telling stories of helping build the walls that are slated to come down in our upcoming remodeling. Parents, teachers and former board members attended, as well as many of the high school kids. It was exciting to have them all there."

The key to this success? Kathie credits the very teens who attend the Center's activities - well-respected kids in the community, who care about the center. When the invitation came from the very kids who benefit from the Center's work, the public responded.

Since that event almost 2 years ago, support for the Center has steadily been rebuilding, and Kathie cites the good feelings folks left with that evening as the genesis of that turnaround.

Bring in Bigtime Dignitaries

For years, Save the Bay in Providence, Rhode Island, has used its annual meeting to bring dignitaries to the very environment Save the Bay is trying to protect. According to Save the Bay's former Deputy Director and now nonprofit consultant Gayle Gifford, the event is a brunch in Newport, right along the Bay. Speakers have included Ted Danson, Jerry Greenfield of Ben & Jerry's, Robert Kennedy, Jr., former NBC news correspondent Garrick Utley, and Vice President Al Gore. Meeting size has ranged from 200 to 1200 guests.

"The Governor of Rhode Island has traditionally welcomed the crowd, which typically consists of the entire Congressional delegation, most of the leading state representatives and senators, many mayors, city council members, commission members, etc., as well as many of Save The Bay's top corporate supporters - presidents of banks, major utilities, etc.

The event is not a fundraiser, but rather a giant member pep rally, thank you party, opportunity to lay out the agenda for the year and reminder to elected officials of the support the Bay has from all parts of the state. Save the Bay's annual meeting has become a place to be seen."

Brainstorm Sheet: _____

❖ Introducing Whole Groups to the Organization via Organized On-Site Events

Volunteer Events:
What work does your organization have that could be accomplished by a large group? Are there projects the board or staff have discussed that have been tabled because it seemed they would require too much work?

_____

_____

_____

_____

_____

_____

Focus Group Event:
List the programs and issues you might address with a Focus Group Event. What questions could you ask about those programs? Who would you invite to the first few events?

1.) _____

2.) _____

3.) _____

4.) _____

5.) _____

6.) _____

Brainstorm Sheet: _____

Sheet Two

❖ Introducing Whole Groups to the Organization via Organized On-Site Events

Annual Meeting:

Who might you invite to an annual meeting event? What sorts of mission-focused events can you think of?

_____

_____

_____

_____

_____

_____

Follow-Up Activities:

After you have connected your organization with your friend, how will the organization maintain that relationship?

3 months after the introduction _____

6 months after the introduction _____

1 year after the introduction _____

2 years after the introduction _____

Each friend represents a world in us, a world possibly not born until they arrive, and it is only by this meeting that a new world is born.

Anais Nin

Making New Friends

Friendship is the hardest thing in the world to explain. It's not something you learn in school. But if you haven't learned the meaning of friendship, you really haven't learned anything.

Muhammad Ali

MAKING NEW FRIENDS

The last section focused on the art of matchmaking, introducing two groups that are already important in the lives of your Board Members - their friends, and the organization they care enough about to spend their time leading and governing.

In this section, we will focus on extending your organization's engagement efforts further out into the community, by getting to know brand new friends - the people your board and staff do not know yet.

The most effective way to meet and engage brand new people is to introduce yourself via advocacy for your mission. Advocacy is all about telling your story and seeking support for the cause, connecting with new friends who care about the issues at the heart of the work your organization does.

If your board is Community-Driven, conscious of being accountable for engaging your community in the mission your organization provides on their behalf, the strategies in this section will become more than just a way to raise friends. They become an imperative, a mandate.

To accomplish that goal, the strategies include three ways to connect with the general public to engage community members with your mission:

- ❖ **Public Speaking**
- ❖ **Public Writing**
- ❖ **Public Affairs Interviews on Television and Radio**

Through these advocacy-based strategies, your Board Members will connect the community with the essence of your organization - the improvement you want to make in your community's quality of life. And that is a big part of what being your organization's ambassadors is all about.

With public sentiment, nothing can fail; without it, nothing can succeed. Consequently, he who molds public sentiment goes deeper than he who enacts statutes or pronounces decisions.

Abraham Lincoln

❖ Public Speaking

The power of public speaking to introduce your mission to new friends cannot be emphasized enough. Public speaking allows you to share your organization's message with a whole group of people - that result alone is of great benefit.

In addition, though, each individual in the audience is a potential friend for your organization. If you have not done public speaking on behalf of your organization, you will be surprised at how many individuals will approach you afterwards, giving their business cards and asking how they can help.

Some people are petrified at the thought of public speaking. Others love it. Either way, there is a role for you in this arena. This section will provide the basics for those who fall into both camps. For more information on the power of public speaking to make huge gains for your organization, see the AfterWords.

Public Speaking Gets the Word Out

During one of the very first Diaper Drives years ago, Dimitri and I were asked to speak at the local homebuilders association. We had about 10 minutes to tell the story, dispelling myths and answering questions as we went along.

After we spoke, Barbara introduced herself, asking how she could help. The result of that one speaking gig almost 10 years ago has been countless diapers collected by the employees in Barbara's workplace; countless volunteer hours by Barbara and her hus-

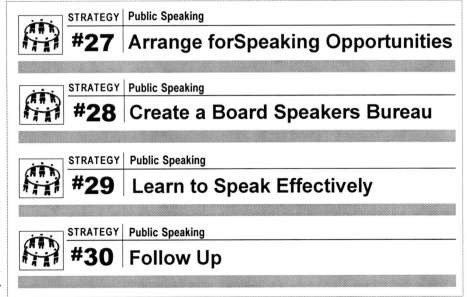

	STRATEGY	Public Speaking
	#27	Arrange forSpeaking Opportunities
	STRATEGY	Public Speaking
	#28	Create a Board Speakers Bureau
	STRATEGY	Public Speaking
	#29	Learn to Speak Effectively
	STRATEGY	Public Speaking
	#30	Follow Up

band; countless dollars in donations she has coaxed from her employer and the sub-contractors she works with; sponsorship on the part of her employer's bank; and the immeasurable passion Barbara now brings to the table as a Diaper Bank Board Member. All that from one speaking gig!

What is Public Speaking?

Public speaking - the words bring joy to some, and make others quake. That is because public speaking often brings to mind the picture of the skinny 8th grade kid, mouth filled with braces, standing alone on a stage, facing the school assembly and thinking, "Please, God, take me now. Death would be better than this."

Relax and read on. Ensuring public speaking is a constant activity for your organization does not mean you have to be the one doing the talking.

Public speaking also does not have to mean addressing a huge audience, although it can. Public speaking can mean talking to a grade school class or a scout troop. Or it can mean addressing a 500 person Rotary Club. If there is a group that can help move your organization's mission forward, public speaking is one of the most effective tools for introducing that mission to all those people at once.

If you like to do public speaking, this is a great opportunity to lend your skills to the organization. If the thought of speaking in public makes you feel like that scared 8th grade kid, use your contacts to arrange speaking opportunities for those in the organization who *do* enjoy this task.

What is the Goal?

The primary goal of public speaking is to connect the heart of your mission with the hearts of the individuals in the audience. At times you may also have additional goals for a particular talk. For example, when Diaper Bank speakers give a presentation during our December Diaper Drive, in addition to raising awareness of the issues related to our mission, we are also hoping the group will agree to collect diapers for us. Always keep in mind that your primary goal is not that one-time donation, but to introduce your mission and engage your audience to create a long term friendship. Any "ask" should simply be one tool among many you use to get your audience involved.*

* For advice on how to "ask" without it seeming like you are asking, check the AfterWords for details about our Speaker Workbook, *"Building Support through Public Speaking: Tips, Tools and Secrets Any Nonprofit Leader Can Master."*

Who Will We Contact for This Strategy?

Looking at your Life List, some individuals spring to mind quickly as likely candidates for this strategy, for example, those who belong to civic organizations such as Rotary, Soroptimist, etc.

However, public speaking is not always that formal. The following individuals may also be able to provide great opportunities for speaking:

- Individuals who have children in school (any level)
- Individuals who work for a large employer
- Individuals who are involved with their congregation
- Individuals who are involved with a club, union or other group that meets regularly

How to Do Public Speaking

Whole books have been written on becoming an effective public speaker. That is not the intent of this section. The intent is instead to show how public speaking can be used by your Board Members to further the goal of community engagement. And that is an effort that can be furthered by both those who love speaking and those who fear it in their very bones.

 STRATEGY **#27** | ### Arranging for Speaking Opportunities

Whether or not you will be the one doing the actual speaking, the most important task you can take on for your organization is to make the initial connections. This is done simply by contacting the individuals you know from civic groups, school PTA's, etc. Arrange a meeting for that individual with your organization's Executive Director (and maybe a tour - check out Strategy #11), and determine what steps are necessary for presenting your organization's story.

As a bonus, whether a speaking engagement comes of this meeting or not, the meeting itself is a great opportunity to make the connection with one more prospective friend for your organization.

 STRATEGY **#28** | ### Create a Speakers Bureau

To create a "speakers bureau," you need individuals with two qualities:

- They must enjoy public speaking
- They must be knowledgeable about the organization.

While this is a great way for Board Members to provide support, your speakers bureau does not have to be limited to Board Members or staff. Individual volunteers, former Board Members, Dream Team members (see Strategy #40) - anyone who enjoys speaking and knows the organization can participate in your organization's speakers bureau.

Most Important: Don't forget to include individuals who have benefitted from your services. Patrons and clients make some of the most powerful speakers, as they speak not only as advocates, but as someone who has directly experienced the benefit your organization provides.

As you will quickly see, the work of the speakers bureau is one area where the ongoing board education noted in Strategy #1 will really pay off. It is helpful also to have an ongoing source of stories - success stories, horror stories, stories that prove points.

One helpful activity is to have an annual speakers planning and training session. This is where Board Members and other speakers will learn new information, new stories, new needs for the organization, all of which can be incorporated into the talks they give. (It may be helpful to include all Board Members in this session. Whether the talk you give is to an audience of 200 or to an individual lunch companion, you should all have the same stories and information to share.)

Your board may also want to create a speaker kit, including information about the programs, the community issues you are addressing, and the stories you will use to show the work your organization is doing. The more you intend to take advantage of this particular strategy, the more you will want to be well-equipped to do the job.

STRATEGY #29 | Learn to Speak Effectively

Effective public speaking is easy if you have done your homework. And that homework should include everything from the choice of topic, to the writing of the talk, to how you present yourself, to how you follow up afterwards.

This topic fills whole books, and there are great books and web resources available that do the job really well. For a list of some resources in that area, check the AfterWords.

In addition to reading and getting resources off the web, don't forget Toastmasters. For those who are not familiar with Toastmasters, it is an organization with affiliates around the world, dedicated to making people into better public speakers. There is hardly a community that does not have a Toastmasters group actively meeting and practicing giving speeches. Just check the white pages of your phone book for one in your community.

Finally, many communities also have leadership development groups, perhaps affiliated with the local chamber of commerce. Public speaking is often a big part of the work done by these groups. In these programs, you will not only gain speaking and other skills, but you will network with other community leaders - the perfect time to brush up your "Personal Advocacy" skills!

AT THE DIAPER BANK

Audrey is one of the Diaper Bank's most effective speakers. Now a woman in a professional position at a local corporation, it was still early in Audrey's work life when her 2nd child was born with multiple complications. As a single mom, the only way she could ensure her son would get appropriate care was to leave her job and care for him herself. She lost her income, living off what she could until her baby was stable enough for her to go back to work. One day, as she was receiving a package of diapers from a social service agency, she asked where those diapers came from. It was then she learned about the Diaper Bank.

We knew none of this. The first we learned about Audrey was when her son was about 3 years old. She showed up at our annual Diaper Drive kick-off, her son by her side. He was carrying a package of diapers almost larger than himself. Audrey asked to talk with the radio DJ who was hosting the day. It barely took a moment for Bobby to know her story belonged on the air.

Audrey had finished her story, when Bobby asked her, "Why are you here today?" And here is what she said: "I promised myself that as soon as I could get back on my feet, I would bring diapers back to the Diaper Bank, for someone else who is in need. You helped save my son's life. I cannot thank you enough." Her son then put their package of diapers onto the pile. And there wasn't a dry eye at the event.

Since that time, Audrey has been an ardent supporter of the Diaper Bank, giving back in many ways - but most importantly as a speaker. As often as she can, she will bring her son with her - a young man now 10 years old. And when she introduces him, there is still not a dry eye in the house.

 **STRATEGY #30** | **Follow Up**

After your talk, individuals will approach, wanting to offer their help. Your board will want to create mechanisms to ensure the business cards you are handed do not fall though the cracks. This can be addressed by having board and staff work together to create a program with logical next steps for those who express interest. This could simply be that within 24 hours of the event, a staff person will follow up with that person, inviting him/her for a tour. Whatever your board decides, as with all the activities in this book, follow-up is the key.

And of course, don't forget to send a Thank You note to the group for extending the gracious invitation for you to speak there in the first place!

What is the Role of the Board Member in this Strategy?

Depending on their comfort zones, Board Members may take one of two roles in this strategy. The first is to help arrange for speaking opportunities. That is something anyone can do, because it is the rare Board Member who does not know at least some small group that can be gathered to hear your organization's story.

For those Board Members who do enjoy public speaking, the role of "speaker" is one of the greatest roles a Board Member can take on. It says a lot about an organization when Board Members are publicly engaged in the community, promoting and advocating for their cause.

AT THE DIAPER BANK

We learned the power of Public Speaking early on in the history of the Diaper Bank. It seemed every time we spoke in front of a group, we would get at least one volunteer, at least one diaper drive started in a kid's school, at least one donation or connection to someone wonderful.

And we learned to never pass up the opportunity to speak, no matter how small the group, or how unlikely the location.

Like in a van traveling down the highway, for example.

During the time when we were transforming our little philanthropic project into an official Diaper Bank, we realized it would be helpful to have a "fiscal sponsor." Rather than form a new tax-exempt organization, with the need for its own bookkeeping systems and its own board, we took the advice of people we respected, and looked to start the Diaper Bank's life by partnering with an already-established larger organization, who could act as the Diaper Bank's 501(c)(3) and watch over the fledgling organization as it grew.

That is when we met Jannie Cox, CEO of Carondelet Foundation. Carondelet Foundation is a local healthcare foundation whose primary responsibility is raising money for 3 Southern Arizona hospitals. Jannie took to the idea immediately. The only thing now standing between the Diaper Bank and the final decision was a presentation to the foundation's board of directors. Here is the call we received at about 3:00 one afternoon:

> "The board would love to meet with you. The problem is they are meeting tonight. The bigger problem is they are meeting at our hospital in Nogales (an hour away). And the biggest problem is we have a packed agenda already. So what would you think of driving down with us in the van? You could give your presentation on the road."

Two hours later, we were on a van to Nogales, telling the story of diapers to the foundation board. By the end of that ride, their answer was, "Yes."

Board Members still remember that van-ride and the stories we told, even after all these years. Of course the years have turned the true story into a fish tale, as Board Members "recall" our commandeering the van, not letting them leave until they promised to take on the project. Knowing our little talk has risen to the status of legend tells us something about the power of seizing every opportunity to tell your story.

Brainstorm Sheet: _____

❖ Public Speaking

Venues for Speaking:

Using your Life Lists as a guide, brainstorm with your board about possible opportunities for speaking.

1.) _____

2.) _____

3.) _____

4.) _____

5.) _____

6.) _____

Topics for Speaking

What are the topics most important to be shared with members of your community? What do you wish everyone in your community understood about your mission? What are biases or mistaken impressions you would like to dispel?

1.) _____

2.) _____

3.) _____

4.) _____

5.) _____

6.) _____

Follow Up

What types of follow-up activities could your organization do for those who express interest after hearing you speak? Who should be in charge of that follow-up?

1.) _____

2.) _____

3.) _____

4.) _____

5.) _____

6.) _____

The act of writing is an act of optimism. You would not take the trouble to do it if you felt it didn't matter.

Edward Albee

❖ Public Writing

Another great way of telling your story and connecting with people who might want to get to know your organization is through writing. Most organizations understand the power of sharing information about their mission in writing, as they watch the effect of their newsletters and direct mail pieces.

But what we are calling "Public Writing" is going beyond your own internal pieces, heading out to the world of writing for public consumption. By writing for the general public, your written wisdom will not just go to those who already know you, but to those who do not know you yet.

Writing your own articles, editorials, letters to the editor and such is effective for two reasons. First, you will have the opportunity to tell your own story in your own words. Second, though, once the article is published, you will have a credible piece to send as a mailing, for use with some of the other strategies in this book.

Strategies for Public Writing include

#31 - #33 Writing for the Newspaper

#34 - #35 Writing for Other Organizations' Newsletters

Writing for the Newspaper

When it comes to the poverty issues addressed by the Diaper Bank, it seems every other day there is an article in the paper to which we want to respond. There was the time the Arizona State Legislature sought to eliminate childcare subsidies to balance the budget, never considering the effect on workforce development and the increase in welfare-related costs for those who, without that subsidy, could not go to work. Or the time a columnist interviewed the last remaining diaper service in our community, where the owner of the diaper service stated that cloth diapers would solve the problem for babies in poverty. (For the record, if a

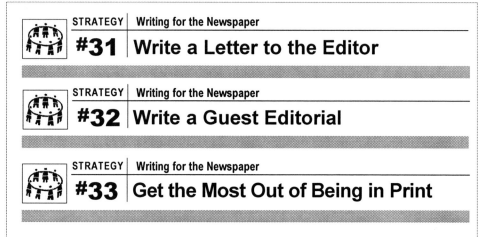

	STRATEGY	Writing for the Newspaper
	#31	**Write a Letter to the Editor**

	STRATEGY	Writing for the Newspaper
	#32	**Write a Guest Editorial**

	STRATEGY	Writing for the Newspaper
	#33	**Get the Most Out of Being in Print**

mom wants to leave her child at a childcare center, most centers require disposable diapers. No disposables, no childcare. No childcare, no work.) Or the time a public interest law group sued the State healthcare system for its failure to provide incontinence supplies to the disabled.

And so we have learned to read the paper proactively, looking for those misconceptions and countering them at every turn. The result is that the Diaper Bank's message is regularly delivered to our community, in our own words. And that message provides multiple avenues for engaging new friends

What is "Writing for the Newspaper"?

When organizations engage in "public relations," their first hope is that the newspaper will cover their story in a positive light. Their next hope is that the story will be reported accurately. With the media, we tend to feel that mixed bag - we want the coverage, but we can never be sure what the media will say or how they will say it.

To ensure the message is one you can use to introduce the cause to new friends, sometimes it is more productive to tell the story yourself, rather than hoping the media will get the story right.

It is likely that on a fairly regular basis, you can find an article in the newspaper that touches your organization's mission in some way. The article may anger you - the reporter has it all wrong. Or you may agree with the point of view of the article (or the person quoted in the article), only to see a deluge of letters to the editor disagreeing. Or you may simply think, as so many of us do, that the reporter missed much of what is truly important about the story.

The opposite situation is unfortunately just as true - where you see an issue so critical and compelling, and the newspaper continually ignores that issue. You never see a thing about that issue in the paper!

If any of these is the case, get out your pen, and let the newspaper know! In the process, you will be reaching out to a slew of prospective friends who care about your cause.

What is the Goal of this Strategy?

There are multiple goals to this strategy, and chances are you will think of even more than the ones we note here. First, you will be communicating about and connecting people with the issues directly affecting the mission of your organization - the definition of advocacy!

Through this communication, you will educate, a big part of the mission of just about every organization.

The mere publication of the letter or editorial piece will add credibility and publicity for your organization.

And for the most part, barring heavy editing on the part of the newspaper, the point of view addressed in that piece will be in your own words.

In addition to all that, you will have copies of this credible piece to send to your friends.

And with all that benefit, you will be engaging new friends around the essence of your mission - a great basis for real friendship.

Who to Contact for this Strategy

Regarding Letters to the Editor, most newspapers provide specific instructions for writing those letters. Typically those instructions are found on the editorial page itself, and will include information regarding length, to whose attention letters should be sent, etc. If you are writing a guest editorial, the contact will be the Editorial Page editor. In a smaller community with a smaller newspaper, that same person might be the editor-in-chief of the whole paper.

And if any of your board members know individuals who work at your local newspaper, that contact can guide you as well.

How To Do It

STRATEGY #31 | Writing a Letter to the Editor

Writing a letter to the editor is relatively easy. Find your newspaper's specifications for length, where to submit, etc. Usually newspapers want to be sure you include contact information, in the event they need to get hold of you to verify you really are who you say you are. (That is a big concern for newspapers, so follow their rules for attribution.)

In your letter, be sure to be courteous, even if you are outraged. While venting may feel good in the short term, in the long run, being belligerent is usually not the best way to engage friends in your issue.

And don't forget to wear your Board Member hat when you sign your letter, signing with your board affiliation, rather than your "professional" title unless that title is immediately applicable. For example, if the letter is about osteoporosis, it might make sense to sign the letter as follows:

> Dr. Herbert Smith
> Director of Gerontology at County General Hospital
> and Board Chair, Our Town's Osteoporosis Awareness Association

If, however, the letter is about funding for the arts, then Dr. Smith's professional life will not mean much. A more appropriate signature might be:

> Dr. Herbert Smith
> Board Member,
> Downtown Arts District

STRATEGY #32 | Writing a Guest Editorial

Writing a guest editorial and having it published is not as easy as getting your letter to the editor published. However, it is not only possible, but such a great tool for your organization's FriendRaising efforts, that it is worth the extra work to make it happen. The following steps will help:

1) Determine what the point of view of the editorial will be. Editorials need a point of view, and if that point of view is potentially controversial, so much the better! Writing a report on 5 ways the arts make our community a better place might work in some cases, but when that same "report" becomes an opinion piece - perhaps "5 Reasons Our City Council Should Not Cut Funding for the Arts" - now you have a point of view!

2) Once you have your ideas firmly in hand, call the editorial page editor, and ask if he/she would be interested in publishing such a piece. Depending on the size of the market you live in, and the size of the paper, you may be instructed to submit your request in writing. Do so. Provide the point of view you have honed, and perhaps a few of your salient points.

3) Once you have been given the go-ahead, write the article. (Or if you have not been given the go-ahead, and instead have gotten the run-around, write the editorial and submit it according to whatever guidelines you can find - most newspapers will provide those guidelines if you ask.)

4) Most editorial pages do not want to see more than approximately 650 words. And if you think writing 650 words about a subject will be easy, just try it! Writing 2,000 words is easy - getting that same point across in only 650 words will take some work.

5) Remember that each paragraph in your editorial should provide a distinct point to support your point of view. A helpful trick once you have determined your overall theme is to make a list of your supporting points. Then write a paragraph for each of those points, showing how that particular point supports your overall theme.

6) If you are rusty at writing these types of pieces, here is an old writing trick you may remember from college essays: Don't worry about writing that snappy introduction until after you have written the meat of your article. Once you have provided all that evidence to make your case, it is far easier to go back and write the introduction - the initial statement of your point of view (Remember the "thesis statement" from your high school writing days?).

7) If possible, use a story to prove your point. You can weave the story throughout the essay, or use it as an example and refer back to it. A story is always a great way to start and end any advocacy communication, as it will "show" rather than "tell" the reader why your point of view is the "correct" one. (And if you have a story that will make them cry, all the better! People respond best when they not only understand an issue in their minds, but feel it in their hearts.)

8) Provide contact information at the end, in your own words. *"Dr. Herbert Smith is the board chair of Our Town's Osteoporosis Awareness Association, and Director of Gerontology at County General Hospital. You can reach the Osteoporosis Awareness Association at www.OTOAA.org or at 909-555-1212."*

STRATEGY #33 | Getting the Most You Can Out of Being in Print

Whether you have written a letter to the editor, or a full-blown editorial, once it has been published, your board's work will have just begun. That is when each Board Member will send that editorial to everyone on their Life Lists, accompanied by a sticky-note that either introduces them to the organization or asks to meet to talk further. This mailing will be about advocacy for the issues of importance to your organization, paving the way to building friendships.

In addition to the people each Board Member personally knows, the board president may also want to send a copy to all the elected officials in your area - Town Council members, County Supervisors, State Legislators, etc. Do not just use a sticky-note for these people (unless you know them personally); instead, write a *brief* letter on your organization's letterhead, letting your elected officials know that you would love the opportunity to talk with them further about this issue. Let the editorial speak for itself by keeping that letter brief - 2 paragraphs, perhaps even one. The letter should just ask for their attention and the opportunity to talk about the issues. Many of these officials will surprise you with a phone call, following up on your letter!

Bonus Strategy:

If you and your Executive Director want to really move to the next level, follow up those letters to your elected officials with a phone call, asking for an appointment to discuss those subjects. Elected officials and their aides are so often bombarded with people who want something from them. By calling when you do not want anything but the ability to share information about an issue they will at some point have to vote on - but not now - you are able to be there as an advisor, not as someone looking for a vote, a favor. End the conversation by letting that official know you are happy to serve as an advisor about these issues if and when the issue ever comes onto their agenda. The worst they can do is ignore that suggestion, and you never know when they will take you up on it!

Whether or not you follow up your letters to elected officials by phone, you will have put your foot in the door with someone your organization will want as a friend - someone who may be in a position to make decisions that affect the issues you care about. And you will have done so with a piece that lends credibility, because whether or not it is true, most people still believe that to write for the newspaper is something pretty special.

What is the Role of the Board Member in this Strategy?

While letters to the editor and editorial essays have an impact when they are written by an Executive Director, the real impact comes when you are writing as a volunteer Board Member - just an average community member who cares. There are two ways to accomplish this, depending on the comfort level of the Board Member.

For Board Members who are well-versed in the issues facing the organization, the Board Member can actually do the writing, submitting the letter or guest editorial, and helping with the follow up work. It is always a good idea to run the letter by the Executive Director for the sake of accuracy, as he/she knows these issues intimately.

However, if you have no Board Members with the level of knowledge to write the piece themselves, you might instead have the Executive Director draft the letter / editorial / article, or create an outline with the specifics. The Board Member can then edit that piece to make it more personal, sign it and send it.

Lastly, be sure to coordinate any letter / editorial writing with the other communications efforts of the organization, to be sure timing and approach of those pieces are working in conjunction with your other efforts.

Friend Raising

Arizona Daily Star

B6 · ARIZONA DAILY STAR / Thursday, May 20, 2004

EDITORIALS & OPINION

Support adult-diaper campaign

By Hildy Gottlieb
SPECIAL TO THE ARIZONA DAILY STAR

As we prepared for the Diaper Bank's "Adult Campaign" this month, I got a call from Andy, a longtime supporter. His words startled me.

"Please don't emphasize the elderly," he said. "Babies have no choice in their poverty, but the elderly have had their whole lives to get their act together. They have no one to blame but themselves."

I took a breath. We receive so many calls like this one, with lists of why we shouldn't help others. After all these years, I've learned just to give the facts.

Callers who start with, "Those people should just use cloth diapers," receive the fact that most child care centers require disposable diapers.

To keep a job to support her family, a mom must leave disposable diapers with her child.

Callers who suggest, "Those people shouldn't have babies in the first place," are reminded the baby is here whether we approve of her/his existence or not, and at this tender age, (s)he is already a youth at risk.

And so I responded to Andy the way I'd responded to those other callers. First I asked him to think of his own mom and dad. Then I gave him the facts.

Fact: If a man worked his whole life, his wife staying home to raise children, a prolonged illness could sap their life savings, leaving his widow nothing to live on.

The average Social Security benefit is $880 a month, and incontinence supplies cost $100 a month, which Medicare doesn't cover.

Fact: Incontinence is one of the leading factors in the elders' being placed in nursing homes. It is a leading factor in otherwise healthy seniors' becoming homebound. And it is a leading factor in elder abuse.

Frustrated, Andy asked, "So what's the answer?" And here's what I told him.

First, we must address the overwhelming immediate need for incontinence supplies. That means helping the Diaper Bank collect and distribute these items to those who need them.

GUEST OPINION

Then, with one out of five adults older than age 65 suffering some degree of incontinence, the next step is to stop whispering about incontinence, and start demanding that Medicare cover incontinence supplies.

A full 40 years after our country declared war on poverty, we must remind our congressional leaders we are not talking about an anonymous face, but about someone's mother or father.

"How would you vote, Congressman, if your own mother hadn't left the house in two years, for fear of embarrassment, all because she couldn't afford $100 a month for supplies?"

And finally, it's time to assemble as a community and as a state, to demand that being No. 48 in the nation in virtually every social indicator is no longer acceptable.

We must demand that our state's leaders aim instead at becoming No. 1. We must demand they ask in every budget decision and every policy decision, "How can our state be the very best place to live? How can we build a community that doesn't need a diaper bank?"

Being No. 1 isn't impossible. Just as there is a No. 48 right now, there is a No. 1 state right now as well. If we only dared ask the right questions, that No. 1 spot could be ours.

For the sake of all our moms and dads, for the sake of the community we are leaving to our children, for the sake of their not needing to beg for incontinence supplies when they are older than 65 — let's aim for being No. 1.

And while we are doing that good work, I hope you will follow the lead of my friend Andy.

He came by the Diaper Bank office the other day. He had a package of incontinence supplies to drop in the bin.

▶ *Hildy Gottlieb is co-founder of the Southern Arizona Community Diaper Bank. For dropoff locations for the "Adult Campaign," head to www.DiaperBank.org*

Reprinted with permission from the **Arizona Daily Star**

Writing for Other Organizations' Newsletters

The Diaper Bank is often featured in the newsletters of both those who are supporting our efforts (employers doing diaper drives) and those who are receiving our services (agencies receiving our diapers). This shared message is just one more way to engage our mission with individuals we would love to call friends.

STRATEGY	Newsletters
#34	A Feature Story

STRATEGY	Newsletters
#35	Highlight an Event

What is Writing for Other Organizations' Newsletters?

If you know someone who is involved with a large organization, then you know someone who gets a company / neighborhood / church / club or other newsletter. These newsletters are often looking for new interesting subjects to share, and that provides your organization with access to one more public venue to connect with potential friends.

What is the Goal of Using Other Organizations' Newsletters?

There are a number of goals for this effort. The most obvious is to raise awareness of the issues your organization is addressing among folks who may want to join forces and help. In addition, though, you can use these newsletters to announce events and other happenings that invite participation. And depending on whose newsletter it is, you may even be able to ask for one or two of the items you noted on your list of needs for Strategy #3.

Who to Target for this Strategy

This strategy will apply to those people on your Life List who have access to a newsletter. That could include:

- People who work for a large employer
- People who are active in their neighborhood association or homeowners association
- People who regularly attend religious services or are involved with a congregation
- People who belong to a club or civic organization

How to Feature Your Organization in Other People's Newsletters

 **#34 A Feature Story**

Depending on the mission of your organization, there are different ways to approach newsletters that are not your own.

In some cases, an employer or congregation might agree to just highlight your organization in a few paragraphs in their newsletter, as a public service or a point of interest to their readers.

In other cases, however, the issues your organization deals with may be directly pertinent to the needs of that employer, congregation, etc. For example, health issues, addiction issues, and other such issues affect employers; if your organization deals with these issues, that may make a natural fit. In such a case, you might ask if your organization can do a monthly Q&A on issues that affect their employees. (Once your organization has 6 or 8 of those under your belt, you may be able to parlay that into a Q&A column in the local newspaper!)

The same approach might work for an arts organization doing a column for the newsletter of local teacher groups, parent groups, religious groups. The opportunities are limited only by your imagination.

Regardless of the content of the article, the point is that it will be written by your organization, so you can be sure the story is told the way you want it told. And it will be circulated by someone else!

This is an easy thing to ask of a friend. "Does your neighborhood association's newsletter ever highlight organizations that can help your neighbors? Can you find out who I should talk to about that?" And it is one more way of extending the reach of your mission.

 STRATEGY
#35 | **Share information about events**

Some internal newsletters, such as congregation bulletins or weekly newsletters for large employers, come out regularly enough to be able to highlight events that would be of interest to that group. Again, this is an easy thing to ask of a friend: "Is it possible your employer's newsletter can highlight our event? Can you find out who I should talk to about that?"

What is the Role of the Board Member in this Strategy?

The most important role for every Board Member in making this strategy work is to connect the organization with possible venues for getting the word out. This is the simple task of asking a friend who works for a large employer, or receives a bulletin from his congregation or union, "Could you find out who we should talk to about having something in your newsletter about the work we are doing?"

Some Board Members are talented writers, and they may want to offer their writing skills for this purpose. In other cases, the article can be written by a staff member. The most important thing a Board Member brings to this activity is the connection with these newsletters.

And as you did with the letters to the editor / guest editorials in the previous section, be sure to coordinate your writing efforts with the organization's other communication plans.

Brainstorm Sheet:

❖ Public Writing

Writing a Guest Editorial

If you are considering writing a guest editorial, list the topics you might write about from a distinct point of view. After each topic, list the supporting evidence that proves your point of view is the correct one. Each topic, with its supporting information, will be an outline for an editorial!

Topic _____

Supporting Information

1.) _____

2.) _____

3.) _____

4.) _____

5.) _____

Topic _____

Supporting Information

1.) _____

2.) _____

3.) _____

4.) _____

5.) _____

Brainstorm Sheet: ────────────

❖ Public Writing

Using Other People's Newsletters

Is there information pertinent to your mission that might be of interest to a local employer? A local neighborhood association? A church group? An apartment complex? A union? A partner community organization / agency? List the groups you might approach to place an article in their newsletter. Next to the group, list the topic you would suggest might be of interest to them.

Group _____

Topics

   1.) _____

   2.) _____

   3.) _____

   4.) _____

Group _____

Topics

   1.) _____

   2.) _____

   3.) _____

   4.) _____

FollowUp

How can you use these written pieces to extend your friendships? Who might you send copies to? How else could these pieces be used as follow-up after they are published?

_____

_____

_____

_____

_____

_____

❖ Public Affairs Interviews on Television and Radio

Being interviewed for television and radio has much the same effect as writing for the public. You will not only be telling your story in your own words, but there are also many other uses for that interview beyond just the audience who will see/hear it when it airs.

While TV and radio can be used in a number of different ways, the focus of this section will **_not_** be on the one minute feature piece we all see on the evening news. While that brief public relations piece may raise awareness as part of an overall marketing plan, it does not provide the time and depth required to begin a real friendship with those who are watching / listening.

This section will therefore focus on introducing your organization to prospective friends via a nice long interview, the kind that is done on Sunday mornings, or on local access channels. And before you say, "But nobody watches those shows!" read on. There are many ways to use this opportunity to meet new friends beyond just the people who happen to catch the show when it airs.

Public Affairs Interviews on TV and Radio

Over the years, the Diaper Bank has received a lot of media coverage. An otherwise normal office, so overrun with diapers that no one can work - well, that visual makes great filler on a slow news day.

With all those interviews over the course of many years, there are two interviews that stand apart from the rest. One is a half-hour show our local Public Access television station shares with the local government channel. The other is a 15 minute radio interview with the general manager of our local Public Broadcasting affiliate.*

	STRATEGY	Public Affairs Shows
	#36	**Telling Your Story**
	STRATEGY	Public Affairs Shows
	#37	**Using the Interview**

When it comes to using the media to really engage folks, rather than just raise quick awareness, there is nothing that compares with having the time to slowly tell your story in your own words.

What is this Strategy?

Before you go into a cold sweat, picturing yourself being grilled by an investigative reporter, relax. This strategy is about doing "feature" news - a "nice" interview about the good work your organization does.

Feature news is the exact opposite of "crisis" news, when life is skidding downhill fast. If that is the case - if your organization is in crisis - the organization should designate one single spokesperson authorized to speak with the media, and that person should be coached by a crisis PR firm in conjunction with the organization's attorney. Seriously. This section is *not* about that.

Unlike the feature news pieces we are most accustomed to seeing on television - the one-minute piece the local evening news might air right before they roll credits - what we are focusing on here is a longer public affairs interview you might see or hear early on Sunday mornings or in other "public service" time slots. These interviews are typically positive, delving into the community issues you want the public thinking about - the importance of the arts, the threat to your local environment, the need for better education, etc. And sometimes they are as long as a full ½ hour!

What is the Goal of Being Interviewed on Public Affairs Shows?

The goal for these interviews will be to engage with those who watch / listen to the show, in a way that connects them to your cause, makes them want to get to know you better. But in addition to introducing your mission to new friends, the interview has the potential for all sorts of other benefits. It can increase exposure and help reinforce your image. It can provide great substance for your website. It can provide a great reason to contact your existing friends, asking them to tune in to the show. It can give you a venue to invite viewers to come to your site, to get to know the organization better. And it can provide you with one more person who may want to help your organization in the future - the interviewer!

Who Should We Target for this Strategy?

While any exposure is good exposure, ideally you will be targeting shows that share the same target audience as you. When you begin this process, do your homework. Ask questions such as, "Who is your audience? What do you know about them?" While you may have already decided that you will speak on any show that will invite you (which is often the best approach, because much of the benefit of this strategy comes after the interview airs), knowledge about the audience will help you tailor what you say to be more relevant to that particular group.

* See the AfterWords to see and hear those interviews.

How Do We Use Public Affairs Interviews to Our Best Advantage?

STRATEGY #36 | Telling Your Story in Person on TV / Radio

First, know that in most markets, talk shows are often looking for good content - not the same old same old, but something new, something their audience will want to know.

Second, this is NOT the place to ask for money. The host may flash your information on the screen, telling people they can call or go to your website for more information, and in many cases, the host will also suggest that those who are interested should send dollars.

But it is not your place to do that ask. After all, you will be "meeting" new friends via the television or radio air waves for the first time. The first step in that relationship will not include having your hand out.

As you set out to engage the listening / viewing audience with the work your organization is doing, the subjects you choose to talk about will be the most effective if they come from the goals of your organization's annual plans. Are you hoping to get the word out to prospective clients, the people who could use your service? Are you hoping to get the City Council or the State Legislature to be more supportive of your issues? Are you looking for collaborative partners for a new program you are launching? The non-money goals of your organization's plans should guide what you talk about.

As you have likely experienced from your everyday conversations with friends from your "real life," people engage more quickly when you tell stories. Therefore, one of the most critical things to carry in your mental bag of tricks is a number of heart-wrenching stories. Regardless of what your organization does, you touch human lives. Tell the stories of the lives you touch.

For more resources for handling a media interview, see the AfterWords of this book.

STRATEGY #37 | Using The Interview Beyond Its Airing

Now comes the advice most of the books and websites will not tell you about "using the media": The biggest value of the interview is not in the people who will see it on TV or hear it on the radio. And given that there is terrific value in the connections made with those watching the show, you can see that this added bonus simply provides more bang for that single interview buck! Here are just a few ways to get more from that interview:

- Send an email announcement to your mailing list, encouraging them to watch the show (or listen on the radio). Tell your existing friends of the critical topics you will be discussing. Whether they watch/listen or not, you have just found a good reason to re-connect with them, to make them feel good about the organization, to make them aware of the issues you are facing, and to let them know that your organization is important enough to warrant that interview in the first place!

- Another credibility builder is to add a section to your website called "Media Watch," where you can list all the shows your organization has been featured on, and all the newspaper coverage you receive. This can be a nice addition to your newsletter as well.

- Bring a volunteer or staff person along to photograph the interview. Use those photos on your website. You can also include those photos in an email telling friends about the show after it happens (or, if it is taped for later airing, announcing when they can see it themselves). You can also use that photo in your newsletter and other communications pieces.

- If the station will agree, ask if you can get a tape of the program, preferably in digital format. If the studio agrees to tape the show, find out ahead of time if you need to bring your own tape / CD / DVD.

  Then ask permission to stream that video or audio on your website. While some stations have policies prohibiting such uses, others will provide that permission, as long as you give them credit - after all, they typically own the copyright to that interview. By noting "Courtesy of Station X" on the piece you use, you will be adding to your organization's own credibility, simply by association.

- Use excerpts of that tape for your organization's video. Again, when it comes to credibility, that portion of the video will show you in a highly credible environment, which carries more weight than just having a talking head telling the story to the camera. Again, give credit to the station who ran the interview.

- When the interview is over, ask the interviewer if you can call him/her if you have future questions about the media. Having a friend at the local tv or radio station is always a plus!

What is the Role of the Board Member in this Strategy?

Not every Board Member is cut out for the job of being interviewed by the media. If you do have a Board Member who is comfortable in that role, and who knows the organization's story well, his/her role should be to accompany the Executive Director, to be interviewed as a team.

Together with the Executive Director, pre-determine the types of topics that would be best for the Board Member to answer vs. the ED - perhaps questions regarding the need in the community, or the response of the business community, or the board's plans for the coming year. And don't be afraid to let the interviewer know beforehand which questions are your strength vs. the strengths of the Executive Director. A good interviewer will want you to look good, because when you look good, he/she will look good, too.

Isn't the ED the Spokesperson? Is this really appropriate for Board Members?

While the organization's Executive Director should be your organization's main spokesperson, by teaming up in pairs to do local public affairs shows, you are able to provide the community side of the organization's story. Nothing is more effective than hearing someone say, "I give up to 20 hours a month to this organization, and here is why..."

AT THE DIAPER BANK

Our community's public access television station does a regular public affairs show called "Local Matters." This ½ hour interview not only airs on the public access channel, but on the City of Tucson's own cable channel as well. The show is one of the most professional of its kind, providing ½ hour for the interview subject to tell his/her story and answer questions.

While the public access and City channels do not have the highest viewership on the cable spectrum, we have been surprised over the years how many people tell us they have seen the interviews. As they cruise through the channels, they see a familiar face, and they stop and listen. We confess, we initially thought, "Well these are people who already know us. How is this helping us raise new friends?"

We soon realized, though, that while these people knew us personally, they did not know much about the Diaper Bank. Invariably they would tell us, "I was glad I watched. I had not known half of what you talked about!" Ü

However, the benefit of those interviews has gone beyond the individuals who saw the show. The benefit has been the ½ hour video we received of that in-depth interview. We have been able to take clips from that video to use elsewhere, and have given copies of the whole tape to new friends who want to learn more.

That one ½ hour show has had multiple ripples for the Diaper Bank. And while we do get some response from those who see the show on tv, the real benefit goes far beyond that one viewing.

* To see that interview, head to the AfterWords for the link to the FriendRaising Web Resource Area.

Brainstorm Sheet: _____

❖ Public Affairs Interviews on TV and Radio

Media Relations

List individuals you know, who work at a TV / Radio station in any capacity, who might be able to help you set up an interview:

_____

_____

_____

_____

Topics to Discuss

What are the topics most important to be shared with members of your community? What do you wish everyone in your community understood about your mission? What are biases or mistaken impressions you would like to dispel?

1.) _____

2.) _____

3.) _____

4.) _____

5.) _____

6.) _____

FollowUp

Consider ways you could use a recording of the interview after it airs. Where could you show it? What could you do with it?

1.) _____

2.) _____

3.) _____

4.) _____

5.) _____

6.) _____

I get by with a little help from my
friends.

John Lennon

PART

3

Asking Friends for Help

A real friend is one who walks in
when the rest of the world walks
out.

Walter Winchell

PART 3 **Asking Friends for Help**

We have stressed throughout this book that a real friend will help your organization in all sorts of ways, sharing an abundance of resources, whether those resources are time, knowledge, connections, dollars, in-kind goods, or the many other gifts we look to friends to provide.

Now that you have engaged friends in the work your organization does, it is time to consider the various ways those friends can help further your organization's mission.

While friendships are not built by first approaching someone with your hand out, once the relationship has been established, asking for help is a natural part of the give and take of friendship. And it is often the case that giving and receiving assistance strengthens the friendship.

Therefore, it is important to remember that the strategies in this section should not be considered until after you have begun to establish a real friendship with the person you will be asking for help. Once your organization has established that friendship, though, the sky is really the limit when it comes to the kinds of gifts your friends will be happy to share.

This section will show you more than just the ways your organization's friends can share what they have, to help you accomplish your mission. It will show you how your Board Members can comfortably engage those friends to provide that help.

If your Board Members have been reluctant in the past to "ask their friends for money," in this section you will start to see the powerful transition that happens when we stop thinking only about money. When we realize the richness of resources our friends can bring to our organizations, we engage those friends in ways that celebrate their own abundance, rather than discounting or even ignoring them because they do not have a lot of money to provide. The more you include everyone in your organization's family, the more you will begin to build an effort the community would not let die. And those are the sorts of efforts every Board Member can feel comfortable participating in.

We hope you will use these strategies as springboards for your own ideas. And please keep us posted. We look forward to hearing from you as you consider new ways to engage your friends in your work.

The approaches in this part of the book include:

❖ Giving Thanks

❖ Asking Movers and Shakers for Help

❖ Asking Businesses for Help

❖ Asking Kids for Help

❖ Asking Congregations for Help

❖ Asking Donors for Help

❖ Asking Other Nonprofit Organizations for Help

Gratitude unlocks the fullness of life. It turns what we have into enough, and more. It can turn a meal into a feast, a house into a home, a stranger into a friend.

Melody Beattie

❖ GIVING THANKS

Regardless of where in the world you live, in virtually every language, there are words for giving thanks. What an amazing thing it is that each of our cultures, all over the globe, acknowledges the importance of appreciating the gifts others share with us.

From the fact that "Thank you" is one of the first phrases taught to small children, to the fact that every major religion emphasizes giving thanks for our blessings, there is nothing as universally gratifying than giving and receiving thanks for the kindnesses others bestow.

#38 | Board Members Giving Thanks

In the Diaper Bank's credo are the following words:
"All parties will be treated with respect, dignity, compassion, grace, integrity, honesty and humanity."

When newcomers read that Credo, often the word that jumps out at them is "grace." We have all been taught to say "thank you" when a friend does something for us. But in truth, we often view saying "thank you" as a chore, rather than an act of grace - something we "have to do" rather than something we feel honored to be able to do.

When someone helps your organization, whatever form that assistance takes, what would happen if you were to *joyfully and often* let them know how much you appreciate both their gift and them?

What is This Strategy?

Being gracious and grateful are a large part of friendship. Therefore it makes sense, before Board Members ask friends for anything, that they first take time to focus on giving thanks.

Frequently saying "Thank you" is delegated to the staff. In truth, Board Members often do not even know whether or when the staff has thanked donors, volunteers, in-kind donors - people who have helped the organization in any way at all.

However, as the volunteer leadership of the organization, Board Members are the perfect ones to offer thanks. That is because the thanks is coming from someone who is also giving of his/her own time and money. "As a volunteer and donor myself, I want to thank you for what you have done." You are a peer.

What is the Goal of this Strategy?

Thanking those who make your organization's mission work possible is the goal of this strategy - thanking with sincerity, with grace - thanking without thinking it is a chore. Saying "Thank you" is one of the most basic rules of friendship.

Thanking in this way benefits both the person being thanked, and the person giving thanks. We assume that when someone is thanked with grace, they will help again and again. And studies support that hunch.

The other half of the equation, though, is that the simple act of giving thanks feels good. When Board Members

---

FOR THOSE WHO WANT PROOF

Casa de los Niños crisis nursery in Tucson, Arizona instituted a program for Board Members to make thank-you phone calls for cash gifts.

Of the donors who were called and thanked by Board Members, 98% gave again, the same amount or more.

Of the donors who did not receive calls, only 61% gave again.

---

participate in thanking friends for their help in making the community a better place to live, the very act of saying "Thank you" can revive Board Members' enthusiasm for the work your organization does. That touch of humanity resonates in all of us.

Who Will We Target with this Strategy?

The target group for this strategy is anyone who has done anything nice for your organization - not just your cash donors, but everyone. The gal who came by with the carload of clothes for your thrift store. The hotel that donated a weekend getaway for your silent auction. The people who spent time at an Interactive Coffee learning about your mission. The friend who arranged a speaking engagement and the scout leader who arranged for volunteers to help with a large task.

If someone has done something nice for the organization, give sincere thanks.

How to Give Thanks

There are a number of ways to thank friends for their help. None is right or wrong, and none is better than another. If you are sincere in your thanks (i.e. not just signing a form letter), that will come through.

Timing

One critical component in giving thanks is timing. Consider the motto regarding cash donations that I first heard used by my friend and fellow nonprofit consultant Debbie Stewart, who advises to "Thank before you bank." Debbie insists that if you have time to take the money to the bank within days of receiving it, you have time to thank the person who sent it.

The same holds true for volunteers who spent a day of their precious weekend helping with your event. It holds true for people who stopped in for a tour instead of heading home to be with their families. If you think of these individuals all as friends, you would certainly call a friend promptly if she had spent her weekend helping you move, or if she had hosted a dinner party you attended. The same holds true for your organization's friends - thank them promptly. That is part of being gracious.

The Personal Touch

The other part of being gracious is to thank people personally. This has nothing to do with the cash receipt organizations are required by government regulators to provide to donors at certain giving levels. While the government does not care if you provide a form letter, your friends will know if your thanks is sincere or not. If friends do something nice for you, be sincere in your thanks by thanking them personally.

Thank Everyone

It is difficult to comprehend the degree to which organizations ignore anyone but their cash donors when it comes to saying thank you. The box on page 125 shares our observations about the ways in which organizations choose to thank (or not thank) their donors, and how they thank them.

But it is worth repeating: Thank everyone. Many boards do an acceptable job of thanking cash donors, only to do no job at all of thanking everyone else. Some organizations only send newsletters to cash donors, making sure to add everyone who sends a check to their newsletter list. But their volunteers? Their in-kind donors? The supporters who connect them up with dignitaries and policy advocates? If they did not send a check, it is not unusual for those individuals to never hear from anyone at the organization unless and until the organization wants something.

What to Do

When it comes to thanking donors, we have seen organizations get Board Members involved in a variety of ways. The point of this section is to emphasize that

    a)   If your board is not routinely saying thank you, they should start doing so, and
    b)   Everyone should be thanked if they have done something nice for the organization, not just cash donors.

The following are just some of the ways Board Members can approach the joyful task of saying "Thank you."

- Have Board Members gather together as a whole board once a month (or however often they can) to do a thank-a-thon, a session where each Board Member is given a list of donors whom they will either call or send a note.

- Have individual Board Members schedule their own times during the month when they can come to your organization individually to do this work.

- Provide individual Board Members with a list of people to contact, and have them commit to make those calls / write those notes within 24 hours. This method is often more convenient for the Board Member, allowing him/her to do the work at home or in his/her office, but it requires a higher level of communication, to be sure all the appropriate follow-up information is entered into the database. It also requires a degree of commitment to actually ensure the calls / notes get done.

As for approaches to saying, "Thank you," there are at least two ways to do this - in writing and on the phone.

- Board Members might write a personal handwritten note on a notecard with the organization's logo. The note can just be a few lines, thanking that friend and telling him how his gift of time or cash or clothes or whatever he gave will be used, as well as why his gift is so important.

- Another way to get Board Members involved in the thanking process is to call friends on the phone, to personally thank them for their gifts. It takes about one minute per call, and often you will simply be leaving a message. But this is probably one of the most rewarding actions a Board Member can experience.

> "Hello, Mrs. Jones? I'm Susan, a Board Member from the XYZ Group. I heard about the clothes you dropped off last week, and I just wanted to call to thank you. Those clothes will mean so much to the women we serve, and I just wanted you to know how much it is appreciated."

That's all it takes. Just a thank you. You may want to make sure each caller has a scripted story about someone the organization helps, in case a real conversation ensues. But in truth, that rarely happens.

That call will mean a lot to the people who make your organization's work possible, because it will be sincere, gracious - it will be what saying, "Thank you" is supposed to be all about!

Important Note:

When you call to say "Thank you," this is *not* the time to ask for more help. This call is *only* about thanking your organization's friends and letting them know how their gift will make a difference. To ask for a gift at this time changes the call to a solicitation. Call to say "Thank you". Period.

"Thank you" calls will not only make your organization's friends feel good. The calls will also be a rejuvenating moment for the Board Member who makes the call. It is one thing to hear reports about numbers of donors and volunteers and other friends - a faceless mass of people who help out. It is quite another to speak with Mrs. Hanlon, who takes a little bit out of her social security check each month to help your organization make a difference.

What is the Role of the Board Member in this Strategy?

The Board Member's role in this strategy is to commit to do this work. While the number of friends your organization has may preclude the board from being able to personally thank each and every one of them, it is important that Board Members take time to express their gratitude to even some of the organization's friends.

Depending on the size of your board and the size of the task of saying "Thank you," you may decide to have each Board Member commit to thanking friends monthly, or have each Board Member commit to do so once a year. Especially during the end-of-year rush, this is a great way for your Board Members to escape the madness of the holiday season and get back to what the "Season of Giving" really means. And as an added bonus, this will be a welcome relief to the staff, who are often inundated at this "crunch" time of year.

A Word About Thank You's for Small Cash Donations and In-Kind Gifts

I remember some years back, a question was posed to one of Charity Channel's discussion groups, asking about the cost/benefit of sending Thank You's to those who donate less than the amount the government requires be acknowledged. The questioner suggested that there is so much effort in responding to every $10 and $15 gift. From a cost/benefit standpoint, is it really even worth the time?

First I picked my chin off the floor, and then responded, trying not to use the words, "Didn't your mother teach you any manners?" Here is what I suggested:

Instead of a Thank You note, why not just send those smaller donors a note saying, "You are too cheap for us to appreciate your gift. It is a bother to process such a small gift, and we really wish you would just go away."

And while few of us would be so bold as to openly suggest small donors are not worth the work that goes into maintaining them on our rolls, sometimes that is how we treat them. Too often we see smaller donors treated like leaves on a money tree; if one falls to the ground (i.e. stops giving), we figure another will grow back in its place. We do not place anywhere near the value on those small donors as we do on our large donors. The large donors, we befriend. Frequently the only thanks a small donor receives is a form letter, followed by our next mailing, asking them to give again.

And given that this is how many organizations treat their small cash donors, we know that in-kind donors are even more frequently treated as if they do not exist at all! When was the last time you received a kind note of thanks, inviting you to take a tour to learn more about the organization, when dropping off a bag of clothes or household goods at the thrift store of your favorite charity?

This is what happens when we measure the value of our friends by the value of their cash donation, without stopping to consider that this is a friend who took time to extend herself to us. Perhaps we should get to know her.

Here is what we often find when we scratch the surface of those small cash donors: Those $5 and $10 gifts from folks on limited incomes are often the gifts that mean the most to the person who gave them. Ironic, isn't it? We lavish thanks on those who give large gifts, when in reality your organization may mean as much or more to the elderly woman who scraped up $10 from her social security check to give to your cause.

When we stop thinking of our donors as donors, and start to see them as friends who care about the work we are doing, that small shift in seeing can truly change everything. When we pick up the phone to call our small cash donors and our in-kind donors and our volunteers, just to say "Thank you," we are telling those friends that we appreciate them as much as they appreciate the work we do.

It is not so much our friends' help
that helps us as the confident
knowledge that they will help us.

Epicurus (341 - 270 BC) Greek philosopher

❖ ASKING MOVERS AND SHAKERS FOR HELP

In every community, there is at least one person, and often more than one, whom every organization wishes they could call a friend. We call these the "If only" people. "If only Ms. Amazing would do a public service announcement for us!" "If only Mr. Wonderful would show up at our event!"

Most organizations have a secret wish list of things they could do if only they had these amazing people on their team. This section will focus not only on bringing those people on board, but on some specific resources such community leaders are often happy to share with community organizations that ask.

Strategies in this section include:

#39   Asking Local Celebrities for Help

#40   Creating Your Dream Team

#39 Asking Local Celebrities for Help

In our community, the Diaper Drive has become one of the most visible charitable campaigns in town. With that visibility has come the ability to rub shoulders with local celebrities, from elected officials to local television and radio personalities to the big-wigs of local commerce. We have been invited by our local congressman to meet the Arizona congressional delegation at the Nation's Capitol. We have shared a stage with John Tesh and other nationally known celebs. It has all been a blast!

But it was not always like that. We did not know a single celebrity, local or otherwise, when we kicked off the Diaper Drive that first year. And every one of the wonderful contacts we have gained since then has stemmed from one single cold fax solicitation, and a lone voice in response.

Shortly after birthing the "Diaper Drive" idea around our conference table, we sent a fax to all the radio stations in town, asking if any of their morning show personalities would consider parking in front of our office, having their listeners drop off diapers on their way to work. The silence in response to that fax was deafening.

Except for one lone DJ.

Bobby Rich from 94.9 MIXfm called to say he thought this might be fun. From that one fax and that one response over 10 years ago, all the rest was born. And none of it would have happened had we not asked that local celebrity for help.

Mr. Big Would Never Help Us...

Because most Board Members do not feel they know people who are powerful or famous, they often get into a mindset that says, "Mr. Big will never help us - we're so tiny!" That could be true, and it could also be the farthest thing from the truth. As we found out with that first fax request for the Diaper Drive, you will not know until you try!

What is the Goal of this Strategy?

We all dream about the wonders of having a local celebrity endorse our cause. Especially if the issue was previously unknown, seeing a local celebrity touting that cause on television can provide instant awareness and credibility.

Local celebrities can help your organization in dozens of ways. They may help by doing a public service announcement (PSA) to be aired on local television stations. They might cut a ribbon at a grand opening, helping to attract media to the event. They can write a letter to your supporters, either thanking them for their assistance or asking for their help. The list of goals is as endless as your imagination. And they are all the things a friend would be happy to do!

Who Should We Target (Aside from the Celebrities Themselves)?

This strategy will target the people on your Life List who come into contact with local celebrities:

- Elected officials (who may be the celebrities themselves!)
- People who seem to know everyone
- People who have lived interesting lives
- Decision-makers at large companies
- Perhaps even members of civic organizations such as Rotary (where the local celebrity might be a member).

How Do We Find Local Celebrities Who Will Help Us?

First, take 15 minutes at your board or committee meeting and brainstorm names of local celebrities you would love to have endorse your cause. Also consider the things those people might be able to help with.

Then have Board Members analyze their Life Lists, specifically with an eye towards those individuals who seem to know everyone in town. If the person who knows everyone in town is *not* already familiar with your organization, then first you will want to cultivate *her* friendship, until she is comfortable enough to share her contacts.

Once that go-between person is already a friend, ask if she knows how you can hook up with Ms. Big. She will tell you quickly if she can help, or if she knows someone who can help make that connection. Be patient if it takes 3 or 4 connections to make this happen, and use that time to educate those 3 or 4 people about the work you do. You can always use 3 or 4 more powerful friends!

Once it is time to meet with Ms. Big, understand that her time is precious. Successful people are busy people. Have your mutual friend do as much of the set-up as possible, and then arrange the appropriate appointments (in person or a phone appointment - a common solution for busy people).

Then make your case, being clear about what you want from Ms. Big. Because this is someone who is used to being asked for stuff all the time, this is one of those rare circumstances where it would not be inappropriate to ask for help on your first visit. While we are still not talking about asking for money, you might request their help with a PSA or some other assistance that involves their presence, and allow them to become engaged with your work by lending a hand.

Note that this is an excellent time to put your Sleuthing skills to work (see Strategy #10). Asking a few well-considered questions (and listening to the answers) can be a great way to build that relationship quickly, making the "asking" part of your trip that much more comfortable. When, in response to one of your sleuthing questions, Ms. Big says, "I might emphasize this side of the issue more than the other," that may be the perfect opening to ask, "Would you consider helping us with a PSA that talks about that part of the issue?"

And just as you would do in a sleuthing interview, don't forget to ask for the names of other people Ms. Big feels might be interested in your work. Getting a referral that lets you introduce yourself by saying, "Ms. Big suggested you might be interested in what we are doing," is priceless.

Follow-Up

Because you will have started this rare relationship by asking for something, it will be that much more important to follow up, to build the relationship into a real friendship. After sending a Thank You for taking time to see you, use a variety of the tools in this book to keep your new friend in the loop regarding the work you discussed with him/her.

What is the Role of the Board Member in this Strategy?

In addition to helping to brainstorm the list of potential bigwigs to contact, the role of the Board Member is to ask his/her friend-who-knows-everyone to make contact with Mr./Ms. Big. And if the friend is not familiar with your organization, it is also the role of the Board Member to use some of the other strategies in this book to bring that friend into the fold!

AT THE DIAPER BANK

One of the most joyful relationships the Diaper Bank has established over the years has been with a man whose face and voice are a household name in our town - a man who is also our town's most publicly and privately generous philanthropist. It took years to establish and build this relationship, but that effort has paid off in a locally famous friend who has lent his money, his name, and his contacts to our efforts, not to mention the volunteer time his staff also gives.

As with any high profile personality, this is not an easy man to get time in front of. We used every connection we could think of - his business associates, his friends. And while we might get a $500 check here or there, that is not what we wanted - we wanted to engage him with the Diaper Bank's mission. We wanted a friendship.

After a number of years of these peripheral contacts (yes, years), both this local celebrity and I happened to be at the same event. A mutual friend was there - someone who had been a big supporter of the Diaper Bank. She introduced us, and Mr. Celebrity shook my hand, saying yes, of course, he knew our work. He started to move on, but my friend stopped him. "You need to listen to what Hildy has to say," she told him. "The Diaper Bank isn't just about babies and diapers. It's about the elderly and incontinence, and all the issues that have to do with that as well."

Mr. Celebrity stopped. He made eye contact with me. And he said two words: "My mom."

Mr. Celebrity and I had an incredible conversation that afternoon. He told me what it feels like to face all the issues he and his mom are facing. We talked together about how many sons are not fortunate enough to have the funds to help their moms the way he can help his.

From that day forward, Mr. Celebrity has personally returned every one of my calls. He has provided generous funding for our most innovative projects. His administrative staff have attended our Diaper Hurling parties and have volunteered to count diapers.

Because of the connection of just one of the Diaper Bank's friends, Mr. Celebrity became a friend - a real friend of our mission. It took 3 years. It was worth every second.

STRATEGY
#40 Creating Your Dream Team

Having developed our manual on Board Recruitment, we are acutely aware of the fact that there are individuals whose input and assistance could be invaluable to your organization, but who just do not have the time to be on your board. Like the local celebrities in the previous strategy, these are often the folks we fantasize and lament about. "If only Mr. Big were on our board, then all our problems would be solved!"

But we really do not need Mr. Big to be on our governing board. Instead, what we need is to be able to count on Mr. Big to use his connections and social status to help the organization when we need it. We need Mr. Big to become part of a team of high-powered friends.

Because the term "Friends of the XYZ Group" has become a euphemism for a fundraising group, we have taken to calling this high profile, highly capable group the "Community Connections Team" or simply the "Dream Team." This group will be the place to engage those people with connections and other high-end abilities, who cannot commit to the time and work it will take to be a full Board Member, but who would be happy to share those resources with your organization.

What is a Community Connections / Dream Team?

The "Dream Team" is a group of friends who can make a phone call, sign a letter, make a connection, cut a PSA, or do one of the many tasks only those with connections or a high profile can do.

This kind of team is often called an Advisory Board, but that term is a dangerous misnomer. First, the misnomer part: the word "advisory" suggests that all you will be asking for is their advice, when in fact you will likely want their help in all kinds of ways.

Secondly, the dangerous part: the word "board" usually connotes some form of power or authority. That often misleads members of the "Advisory Board" into thinking they actually have either some power or some authority, when, in fact, they have neither. With that, it often becomes hard to engage the "Advisory Board" as a group, or difficult to figure out what their role should be, without encouraging them to believe it should be more than it really is.

If you do not like the names "Dream Team" or "Community Connections Team," find a name that makes both the board and the team members feel comfortable. But the important thing is to find a name that is descriptive of what they will really be doing for your organization, and to never call them a "board."

What is the Goal of this Strategy?

The goal of this strategy is twofold. First, the strategy will provide those movers and shakers who do not have time to serve on your board with the opportunity to share what they do have, on an as-needed basis. By creating a way for them to serve your mission without committing large blocks of time, you meet their needs **and** yours, another sign of a true friend.

Secondly, however, the strategy's purpose is to give your organization a high powered, high profile group you can not only ask for favors, but you can promote as supporting your organization.

Who Should We Include in this Strategy?

This strategy will include anyone on your Life List who either has the potential to be a Dream Team member him/herself, or who comes into contact with such individuals. That would include

- Elected Officials
- People Who Seem to Know Everyone
- People Who Have Lived Interesting Lives
- Decision-Makers at Large Companies
- Members of Civic Organizations such as Rotary
- Former Board Members

In addition, you may want to make a list of those individuals you would love to have on your Dream Team. The list may simply include local big-wigs, or you might also look for specific skills. Are you looking for an attorney who can provide pro bono advice about nonprofit issues, but who, due to conflict of interest issues, should not sit on the board? (Having an attorney as a Board Member is always potential for conflict of interest, as that attorney would be representing herself if she gives the board legal advice.) Or are you looking for contacts in a specific profession for a specific project? You might consider adding those areas of expertise to your Dream Team wish list.

How To Create a Community Connections "Dream" Team

The task of assembling the team is simple: Using some of the other strategies in this book, get to know those people who might make great Dream Team members. Then, once you have already met with them and have asked if you can follow up with them, call and ask if they will be on your Dream Team.

Explain:
1) This will require virtually no time commitment, and
2) You just want to know if you can count on them to help if you run into a brick wall on whatever topic you have found you are mutually interested in.

One interesting way to give your organization's Dream Team a bit of prestige is to make this an annual appointment. This makes each year's Dream Team something special, providing special plaques thanking them for their service for that particular year. Further, when you are first asking for their assistance, it sounds less onerous to the person being asked if you can say, "There are no meetings, no commitments other than to make a phone call, sign a letter, or give some advice, *and* it will only last a year! And here is who else has signed up for this year's Dream Team..."

The added bonus of making this an annual commitment is that each year you can announce the appointment of "This Year's Dream Team" in the local press. By making it an annual appointment, each year will bring a whole new group (even if it is, in fact, the same old group) when it comes to announcing it in the press!

What is the Role of the Board Member in this Strategy?

The first role of the Board Member in this strategy is to make the initial connection. The more important role is to do what it takes to maintain that friendship until it has become clear that it is time to hand over the relationship to the staff. That could mean writing a personal note on the newsletter you send to Mr. Big. Or it could mean sending a copy of a newspaper article you feel Ms. Grand might find interesting. The job of Board Members in this strategy cannot be overstated, because even though a Board Member might not feel he is in Ms. Grand's league, as a community member and volunteer Board Member of your organization, that Board Member is more a peer of Ms. Grand than the Executive Director is. And that makes it the board's job to represent the organization to your community's leaders - like Mr. Big and Ms. Grand!

AT THE DIAPER BANK

The overwhelming need for diapers among vulnerable populations, combined with the impacts of not having those diapers, led Dimitri and I to change our whole lives to create not just one, but two Diaper Banks. As we all know, when one is born again, whether to a cause, to a religion, or to quitting smoking, that cause becomes your life. And so, over the years, Dimitri and I have talked about the need for diapers to anyone who will listen. Often that person is a local big-wig, whether we are meeting at a community function, or being introduced one on one through a mutual acquaintance.

We realized how that level of personal advocacy had made a difference in our lives when our radio sponsor wanted to do a live radio play to benefit the Diaper Bank, using local celebrities as the cast. And while one would think the radio station would have connections the Diaper Bank could benefit from, the exact opposite happened. Their staff contacted us, asking, "Could you help us get the Mayor? Our congressman? The sports announcers for the University Basketball team?"

It was then that we realized the Diaper Bank had accumulated its Dream Team, even if that had not really been our intent. These were all people who had toured the Diaper Bank, donated their money and their time, made connections - done everything and more you would want a Dream Team to do. And they are now also the folks who have been willing, year after year, to stand on a stage, acting out parts in the radio play.

From the day we came to that realization, we have been creating our Dream Team with more intent. We have brainstormed who would be likely candidates, and we have begun approaching them to ask for their support. We have been surprised at the connections we did not even realize we had. And we have been pleased at how willing they all are to help.

Brainstorm Sheet: _____

❖ Asking Movers and Shakers for Help

List people you might want on your Dream Team. What skills do they bring? What skills do you need?

1.) _____

2.) _____

3.) _____

4.) _____

5.) _____

6.) _____

List local celebrities you wish were helping your cause in some public way.

1.) _____

2.) _____

3.) _____

4.) _____

5.) _____

6.) _____

❖ ASKING BUSINESSES FOR HELP

When nonprofit leaders think of befriending the business community, typically the first (and often only) thing they think of is asking for a large cash donation. On its surface, this approach seems logical to nonprofit leaders. After all, isn't "business" where the money is?

Unfortunately, the truth is different from the assumptions we make. Donation decisions from businesses are business decisions, based on business circumstances unrelated to the value your charity provides. There are often a zillion reasons that large businesses cannot provide a sizable cash gift to your organization, and just as often, none of those reasons is directly related to your organization. It is just the business of business.

But friendship - well that is a different story! When we have built a friendship with the owner of a small business, with an employee at a large firm, with a local CEO - we have begun to tap into all the other various types of resources only a friend can offer. When approached from the perspective of friendship, your friend will be able to focus on the abundance of what his company does have to offer, rather than lamenting how little cash his business has to spread among "competing" organizations.

Using the approaches in this section, virtually every Board Member will see opportunities for bringing at least one business partner into your organization's family. Once they are part of the family, you will find all kinds of ways to ensure the relationship is ongoing and meaningful for both your organization and your new friends.

Strategies in this section include:

#41 - #48	Asking Small Businesses for Help
#49 - #53	Asking Employee Groups for Help
#54 - #56	Asking Decision-Makers at Large Employers for Help

Asking Small Businesses for Help

Being small business owners whose philanthropic giving-back-to-the-community became the Diaper Bank, we are partial to the work small business owners do to make their community a better place. The first diaper drop-off locations in our community were the small businesses we frequented - the pizza place, the dry cleaner. Our first "employee diaper collections" came from small businesses - a motorcycle shop, a real estate office. While small businesses typically must pinch every penny to survive and to compete with the big guys, they also have the flexibility most large firms do not - the owner is right there and can make a decision on the spot, without having to clear it with anyone.

	STRATEGY	Asking Small Businesses for Help
	#41	**Donating Change**
	#42	**Lunch Room Opportunities**
	#43	**Tagging Advertising**
	#44	**In-kind Gifts**
	#45	**Volunteers**
	#46	**Trade Associations**
	#47	**Business Promotions**
	#48	**Bag Tokens**

What is this Strategy?

If you ask small business owners to help your organization, their first response often reflects the same perception so many of us hold - that the only businesses who can help your organization are the Big Guys.

Here is the truth, though: Small local business owners are typically more willing and able to share a variety of resources with an organization they care about than the big companies. Small businesses are rooted in the communities where the owners' kids go to school, where the causes are personal. For small business owners, helping your organization is a way to participate in making the community they love a better place for themselves, for their families, for their customers.

Small businesses typically have an abundance of assets and resources they do not even think of as assets. By asking them to help with whatever it is they do have to offer, you are helping them as well - helping them see the wealth of resources they are likely not seeing as such.

What is the Goal of this Strategy?

The breadth of goals for which this strategy can strive is limited only by your imagination. Exposure. Volunteers. In-kind support. Cash donations from customers. Small businesses can be flexible and creative to provide anything you can imagine a friend helping with.

Who Should We Target for These Strategies?

Using your Life List, anyone who owns a small business would be the target audience for these strategies. And if you own a small business yourself, it will first apply to you!

Two reminders:

First, this is NOT an invitation to just cold-call a whole strip of small businesses. Remember that the key is friendship and real engagement, first and foremost. Talk to the businesses where you already have a relationship - the place you stop to get your coffee every day, the guy who owns the newsstand or the dry cleaner, the gas station owner who is always so pleased to check your oil.

And second, remember that the important thing is not a relationship with you, but a relationship with your organization. If the gas station owner does not know your organization, you will want to talk with him about the organization to familiarize him first, using the Personal Advocacy approach (Strategy #7). You will find that where you might have been uncomfortable asking for "stuff" before, once you have shared stories, introducing the business owner to the organization over time, you will be less uncomfortable when it comes time to ask for something. (That is the power of Personal Advocacy - when the time is right, you have already been telling the story to everyone you know!)

How Can Small Businesses Help Our Cause?

The following strategies are just a start. What you will find as you read through these approaches is that they do not cost the business a lot, and they do not require a lot of work. While some of these activities may provide a slow, yet steady trickle of support, and others may accomplish something major, all will be relatively simple for a small business owner to say "yes" to, making it easy for your organization's friends to share what they do have, to help out the cause.

STRATEGY #41 | Donating Change

We often see change jars at cash registers for one cause or another. Depending on the business, that cause at the register could be yours!

> **Extra tip:** If the business is yours, and you are often behind the register, it is easy to ask customers, "Would you like to donate your change to The Environmental Cooperative?" This encourages folks to give. It also has the added bonus of providing the opportunity to talk with the customer who responds, "I'm not familiar with them." If this approach could work for you, keep a handful of brochures with your change jar, encouraging people to give and learn more.

STRATEGY #42 | Lunch Room Opportunities

- Keep a change jar in the lunch room, to encourage employees to empty their change.
- If the lunch room does not have vending machines, purchase a case of candy bars / snack items at the local warehouse market, and ask for "Donations: $1 apiece." At about 3pm, those snacks will look really good to the employees, and your organization will benefit.

STRATEGY #43 | Tagging Advertising

If the business advertises on local radio or tv, they might consider taking a few seconds of that advertising time to promote your organization. It takes very little to add a few words at the end of a 30 second spot, such as, "ABC Company urges you to keep our rivers clean by giving generously to The River Group." The impact of that added awareness can go a long way for your organization, and it continues to reinforce the friendship each time that business owner hears it, and each time his customers comment on it.

 STRATEGY **#44** | In-kind Gifts

Depending on the type of business, and depending on the organization, there are often ways a small business can provide far more value than a cash donation, simply by giving what they already have or already do.

Consider the hairdresser who provides free makeovers for women undergoing chemotherapy. The used book store that teams with the elder-housing group, to keep a rotating library at the facility. The contractor's office with ties to a local blueprint shop, for providing free posters for an event. There are all sorts of assets most small businesses do not even realize they have (including and especially their vendor relationships), that could provide benefit for your organization.

STRATEGY **#45** | Volunteers

One of the best "team building" activities a business can do is to chip in and help others. If there is a volunteer activity your organization needs to do (Move to a new office? Paint the existing office? Get the weeds out of that back lot? Get a 10,000 piece mailing done?), getting together with a group of small business employees is a great way to get the job done. The side benefit is not only the "team building" effect for the employees, but the ability to translate that one-time connection with the organization to a longer term commitment. And as an added bonus, once the group members have seen for themselves how important the organization's work is, they may be more likely to put their change in that jar in the lunch room!

And don't forget: These groups of employees are also great groups to invite to a Volunteer Event (see Strategies #21 - 23).

STRATEGY **#46** | Trade Associations

Many small business owners belong to trade associations or other business groups. These are excellent venues for public speaking or other activities to benefit your organization.

When you hear a friend say, "I have a meeting with my trade group this week," find out if there is an opportunity to share your mission with all those people who might help in the same way your friend is helping.

STRATEGY **#47** | Business Promotions

If a business is already devoted to a cause, and already excited to help, a true win-win comes from using that cause in their marketing. The easiest way to do that is for the business to share with the organization a portion of the sales proceeds from a specific promotion.

- A pizza shop might advertise, "This month, for every pizza you order, we will give 25¢ to Homes for Dogs."
- An apartment complex might advertise, "This month, we will give $10 from every new rental to the Family Counseling Agency."

There is always a way to give a portion of sales to a worthy organization. That portion can be large or small, based on all sales or a specific item, for a short term or forever. The critical point is that this effort will help the business and help your organization at the same time.

 **#48** Bag Tokens

Retailers who might normally put the customer's purchases in a bag can reward customers who do not want the bag by donating a few cents - the cost of the bag - to your cause. A small bookstore in our hometown chooses a different charity every month, generating $25-$30 for that charity. That may not seem like a lot of money, but it is a great way for your organization to more deeply engage those business owners. How is that? Each time someone says, "I don't need a bag for that," they will be told, "Thanks - we'll donate the cost of that bag to the Arts Collaborative!" When the customer says, "I'm not familiar with them - tell me about them," it will be the store owner sharing your story, re-committing himself each time he tells it.

What is the Role of the Board Member in this Strategy?

If a Board Member owns a small business, the role of the Board Member will be to determine how your business can assist the organization directly - either with these activities or others specific to your business. Board Members who own small businesses and do participate in this way are also in a great position to encourage other small business owners - friends, individuals they know through trade associations or networking groups - to do the same.

Board Members who do not own a small business can work with the small business owners on their Life Lists, introducing them to the organization. Once those business owners are familiar with the organization, depending on your comfort level, you can be the one to help them find ways to help, or you can work with the Executive Director to do that part of the job.

Again, the exciting thing about this strategy is that it gives small business owners the opportunity to give what they do have to share, rather than feeling inadequate at how little they perceive they have to give. In reality, they have an abundance to share with your organization. The job of your Board Members and Executive Director is to help them uncover all those assets and resources. You will find that this becomes one of the most energizing activities you and your business-owner friends can engage in.

AT THE DIAPER BANK

Small businesses have been part of the backbone of the Diaper Bank's success. Some of the work they do is highly public, bringing traffic to their stores during our high-profile December Diaper Drive. And some of it is completely behind the scenes, done simply because the business owner cares about the cause.

The Diaper Bank created a sponsorship level specifically to allow a small business to participate in the publicity generated by the Diaper Drive. While a tiny mom-and-pop business may not be able to afford a $5,000 radio campaign, they can usually afford $250 that provides them with the tools to be considered an "Official Drop-Off Location" during our December campaign. Over the years, a pizza restaurant has provided its customers with a discount if they bring in diapers, and a stuffed animal store has entered diaper donors into a drawing for whatever bear was popular that year. A self-storage facility offered new tenants ½ off their first month's rent if they brought in a package of diapers or a cash donation for the Diaper Bank.

On the other side of that equation are the folks who receive no benefit from their gift, other than knowing they have done something good. When Pioneer Plumbing heard we needed volunteers with pick-up trucks to help haul diapers during Diaper Drive, they called to offer not only their trucks, but their plumbers! "Our plumbers are always running all over town. Let us help!" For the whole month-long Diaper Drive, you could see Pioneer Plumbing's trucks, filled to the rim with diapers.

And that bookstore that makes a donation each time someone doesn't need a bag? When they handed us our $30 check, they told us how excited their customers were that the store was supporting the Diaper Bank. "Our customers were especially interested in the issues of the elderly - we are really glad you are focusing there." They had been telling our story all month!

It is not an exaggeration to say the Diaper Bank could not accomplish what it has accomplished without the support of our community's small businesses. By sharing the many resources they have to offer, both those businesses and the Diaper Bank's programs are stronger.

Asking Employee Groups for Help

As happens so often in life, we learned about the power of employee groups by accident. In Year 2 of our December Diaper Drive, we sent a mailing to the top 200 employers in our community. Our naive intent was that those companies might consider a donation of diapers. Instead, our mailer was repeatedly handed to groups of employees, and a staple of the Diaper Drive - the employee campaign - was begun. But we also learned that the value of those relationships extend far beyond that one month campaign to collect diapers.

What is this Strategy?

A community's large employers are a great place to build relationships for your organization's mission - not because they are large corporations with deep pockets, but because they often have employee groups who volunteer or raise funds or invite speakers to visit a few times a year. Some companies provide assistance and encouragement to these employee groups, while others provide employees with company time to convene for their community efforts.

	STRATEGY	Asking Employee Groups for Help
	#49	**Speaking Opportunities**
	STRATEGY	Asking Employee Groups for Help
	#50	**Volunteers**
	STRATEGY	Asking Employee Groups for Help
	#51	**Donations of Goods or Cash**
	STRATEGY	Asking Employee Groups for Help
	#52	**Program Advice**
	STRATEGY	Asking Employee Groups for Help
	#53	**Follow Up with the Boss**

What is the Goal of this Strategy?

This is another opportunity to ask groups of individuals to share what they have. As happens with real friendships, the goals of these activities will depend on how the employee group wants to get involved. By tapping into the abundance of resources employee groups have access to, you are engaging these individuals with your mission.

Who Should We Target for These Strategies?

This strategy will apply to the people on your Life List who work in an organization with many other employees - a large company, government, public safety employees, etc.

How Can Employee Groups Help?

Employee groups are often among the most enthusiastic volunteers and donors in a community. A camaraderie occurs when teams of employees who work together by day also offer their assistance together in their off hours.

It is important to remember, as you approach these groups of employees, that each of the employees is wearing two hats. Yes, they are all representatives of the company they work for. But they are also community members who love their community. They want to find ways to help make their community a better place to live. Part of your job is to help them find ways to do that!

The first step will be to use some of the strategies in the previous sections of this book to introduce your organization to your contact with the employee group. Once you have done that, you and your organization's new friend can work together to determine what approaches will make sense for his/her particular organization.

STRATEGY #49 | ## Speaking Opportunities

The first step in generating enthusiasm for your organization's work is often a brief talk at an employee meeting. There may only be 6 people on the official "Employee Team," but depending on the size of the organization, those 6 people may represent several hundred or more employees. These employee representatives are the ones who will bring your story back to the rest of the workforce, so be sure you have made your main points clear enough for those individuals to re-tell them. And make sure you leave them with a poignant and memorable story around which they can rally the troops!*

 STRATEGY #50 | ## Volunteers

If you have a volunteer activity, employee groups are often a great source for volunteers. Use the volunteer activity as you would in Strategies #21 through 23, following up with photos and thank you's.

STRATEGY #51 | ## Donations of Goods or Cash

Some employee groups will collect goods or cash for your organization at specific times of year. Some adopt one charity to help throughout the year; others rotate their support to a different charity each month; while still others save their giving for holiday time. Again, each company will be different, with different approaches, different programs, and different rules for those programs.

STRATEGY #52 | ## Program Advice

Depending on the nature of your mission, employee groups could be an excellent place to go for advice on the very programs you provide. Using some of the strategies from other parts of this book (particularly the Community Sleuthing and Focus Group approaches in Strategies #10 and #24), employee groups are an untapped pool of advisors regarding everything from workplace issues surrounding addiction to increasing educational opportunities for underprivileged kids. Again, groups of employees are not just volunteers or donors - they are community members who care.

STRATEGY #53 | ## Follow Up with the Boss

A big part of thanking the employees is giving them a boost with the boss - the CEO, the regional president - the person in charge of the operations in your community. Even if your only contact has been with the employees themselves, it is that local decision-maker who is, through his/her policies, making it possible for that group to help you. A huge "thank you" to that decision-maker is therefore in order!

This is an important step regardless of what kind of assistance the employees have provided. For example, if the effort was a volunteer project, send copies of the photos to that regional decision-maker - the "boss". Invite him/her to tour your organization, or to meet with you to learn more. He/she may not respond, but if you do that every time the group volunteers, sending photos and thank you's, you will be surprised at how that builds those relationships, even if you get no response. On that day, perhaps years from now, when you *do* need to talk with that decision-maker, it is far more likely he/she will remember your organization and be willing to meet - and his/her assistant will also remember you, and will likely be more amenable to facilitating the appointment.

Your offerings of thanks, complete with photos, will mean that your call is no longer a cold call. Even if you have never exchanged a single word, you will have already begun to establish the relationship. (And if you include that local decision-maker on your newsletter list, with a personal note; if you invite her to your annual meeting event or a volunteer event; if you target her for some of the other activities in this book - well, all that just adds to that relationship building effort!).

* For more on using speaking to help your organization, see the resources in the AfterWords.

What is the Role of the Board Member in this Strategy?

By asking friends who work at large places of employment how your organization can become a beneficiary of that company's employee volunteer group, the Board Member will have made that critical first connection. The Executive Director or other appropriate staff member will then be the logical person to follow up with that contact person.

AT THE DIAPER BANK

Over the years, the Diaper Bank could not name a more loyal group of volunteers than the Volunteer Team at Tucson Electric Power. Starting that very first year of hurling diapers off our balcony, the TEP crew has been a huge part of the Diaper Bank's success. And many of those volunteers have become friends of the Diaper Bank in their own right, outside their work role.

"Diaper Don" Livingstone is just such a friend. Don went from leading the TEP Volunteer Team's efforts, to being an integral part of virtually every diaper sorting effort the Diaper Bank does (whether the TEP crew is there or not) - to now sitting on the Diaper Bank's board of directors! We never would have met Don if it were not for the relationship the Diaper Bank built with Tucson Electric Power.

The relationship with Tucson Electric has also meant employee diaper drives at TEP's workplace, where the employees have collected as many as 15,000 diapers at a time. And it has meant the employees voting to provide a $10,000 grant to the Diaper Bank, from a pool Tucson Electric calls its "Grants that Make a Difference."

The important thing to remember is that employer groups are just that - groups of individuals whose relationships need to be nurtured like any other. The Rules of Friendship must apply to all our friends! We therefore knew the relationship with TEP had attained the status of "true friend" when we received a call from Diaper Don a few years back, asking if Tucson Electric could borrow some palette jacks from our warehouse. It seems they had a project that could use some extra help. How wonderful it felt to know we could give back to folks who had given so much to us!

Asking Decision-Makers at Large Employers for Help

Diapers and CEOs - there's got to be a link, right? In fact, there is. What we quickly found out about CEOs and other decision-makers is that they are people first, and employers second. Starting with our bank (a large national institution), we worked our way throughout the community, extending a hand and then nurturing relationships with key decision-makers at our community's largest employers, engaging them first with the Diaper Bank's mission and the community issues the organization addresses. Through those relationships, we have found sponsors and donors and passionate supporters with tremendous resources that have helped the Diaper Bank for years.

	STRATEGY	Asking Decision-Makers at Large Employers for Help
	#54	**Corporate Employee Gift Match**
	STRATEGY	Asking Decision-Makers at Large Employers for Help
	#55	**In-kind Donations**
	STRATEGY	Asking Decision-Makers at Large Employers for Help
	#56	**Event Sponsorship**

What is this Strategy?

When we talk about decision-makers at large places of employment, we are not talking about CEOs of Fortune 500 companies. Instead, this strategy is all about connecting with local officers with control over a small realm of decisions that could help your organization. The decision-maker could be a community relations representative, a division manager, or a government department head. The layers of decision-making are as different as the names of every large employer in your region.

What is the Goal of this Strategy?

As with the previous set of strategies, the goals for working with these decision-makers will be different depending on the company and depending on the strategy. But equally important as those individual goals, this strategy can also help you connect with an individual who may become a personal friend of your organization, in addition to helping out in his/her capacity as a local community leader. And it never hurts to have friends in high places! (See Strategies #39 and #40 for more on that!)

Who Should We Target for This Strategy?

Use your board's Life Lists to identify individuals your Board Members know, who are decision-makers at large employers in your community.

How These Decision-Makers Can Help Your Organization

In addition to the strategies on the previous pages (regarding tapping into volunteer pools and other resources at large places of employment), the following may also add possibilities to your thinking.

Before approaching the decision-maker for help, however, the first step will be to use some of the other strategies in this book to engage this new friend with your organization's work. If your friend is as creative as some of the decision-makers we have worked with, you may want to make sure to set aside a bit of time for brainstorming, using a sleuthing approach when you first get together. You may be surprised at the creative ways your friend finds to use the resources at his/her disposal, in addition to his/her own personal wisdom and expertise, to benefit your mission.

#54 | Corporate Employee Gift Match

Some companies provide corporate matches for employee gifts to charity, and this is particularly the case with larger companies. In other cases, however, a department head or other person with spending authority can authorize a match up to a certain amount. Therefore, if you are considering asking for employee contributions, it is always a good idea to ask your decision-maker friend if it is possible the company can match those gifts up to a certain amount.

#55 | In-kind Donations

The list of things your organization needs (Strategy #3) likely contains items local companies could help provide. Does the company have an in-house print shop that could help with printing? Are their trucks idle at times, to help move your office, or make a delivery after a massive goods collection? Perhaps they have a graphics department that can spare a volunteer? Until you sit down and talk about what you need and what they have, you never know how the resources at a large company can help.

#56 | Event Sponsorship

Sponsorship is not a donation; it is a marketing tool. Through sponsorship, a company provides support in exchange for publicity. The support can be monetary or it can be in-kind, but the thing that separates "sponsorship" from a straight donation is that sponsorship's purpose is 100% about exposing the sponsor to a target audience to whom they hope to sell their products or services.

It is critical to understand that "Sponsorship = Marketing" when you approach a corporation about sponsoring an event. The key question you must be able to answer will therefore have more to do with how your event will help that company sell its product, than why your cause is so wonderful.

For example, regardless of your organization's mission, if your event will have 100 golf enthusiasts in attendance and your friend is the regional decision-maker for a sporting goods chain, he may want to sponsor that event, providing store coupons to attendees. The sporting goods chain may not care about child abuse or the arts or whatever your cause is, but they may feel a target audience of 100 golfers with money enough to buy a ticket to the event is a worthwhile marketing investment.

Sponsorship decisions are often made by decision-makers out of town, as national marketing firms handle the marketing for most large corporations these days. If that is the case, it is often more difficult to make a case for a local cause, and as a regional manager, your friend's hands may be tied. However, if sponsorship decisions can be made locally, those local decision-makers will be the ones deciding if your event is a fit for their business needs.

Know that sponsorship is not an easy sell, regardless of how logical you think the fit is. Companies keep a tight reign on their marketing dollars, and you are just one of many organizations pitching them with events. So be patient, and keep the ideas in front of your friend the decision-maker. You never know when you will have the right idea at the right time for that company.

What is the Role of the Board Member in this Strategy?

The Board Member's role in building the relationship with the decision-makers at large places of employment is to make the introduction and grease the wheels. Decision-makers in these settings are difficult to get in front of, and difficult to stay in front of. Just because you have made the introduction once, you may be called upon by the staff to get a phone call returned, etc. In this circumstance, the Board Member should plan on continuing to play matchmaker until the relationship has clearly been transformed from a relationship between 2 individuals (the Board Member and the decision-maker) to a relationship between your organization's cause and that decision-maker and his/her organization.

Again, it is important to remember that these individuals wear two hats - that of company representative, and that of community member. By helping them see not only the cash-resources but also the various non-cash resources their company might lend to your organization's efforts, they are empowered to think beyond the scarcity mind-set ("I'm really sorry - we are having a tough year. We wish we could do more...") and out towards the abundance mind-set. And when that happens, both your organization and their firms are the winners!

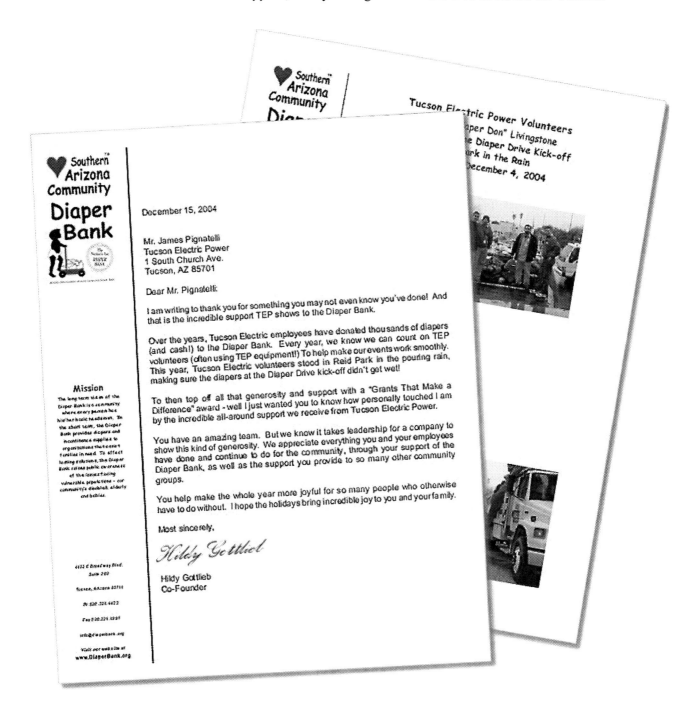

After all the help our friends at Tucson Electric Power have given the Diaper Bank, the letter we sent their CEO included photos of the TEP crew working at our event.

Brainstorm Sheet:

❖ Asking Businesses for Help

Create a "How Your Business Can Help" Fact Sheet

A fact sheet makes it easy for businesses to immediately know how they can help your organization. Fact sheets are also great handouts for speakers who are addressing any kind of civic, employee or networking group.

Using the ideas in this section, as well as other ideas your board and staff generate, create an idea list for how businesses can help your organization. Put that list on your organization's letterhead, and title it **"Simple Things Your Business Can Do to Help Our Organization."**

And don't forget - every communication with those who could help you should include your mission statement.

Note:

While this fact sheet could be created by staff and simply provided to Board Members to distribute to friends, this activity is far too much fun and far too inspiring to leave Board Members out of the process. And besides, many of your Board Members will bring the real-world perspective of what businesses can do, that the staff may not have considered on their own.

How Can Businesses Help Your Organization?

_____

_____

_____

_____

_____

_____

_____

_____

❖ ASKING KIDS FOR HELP

Most everyone talks about the fact that kids are our future, that there is a need to teach them to be involved in their community at an early age. Therefore, engaging with your community's children is the road to some of the most rewarding and long term friendships you can build.

Getting kids involved in your organization's mission can accomplish multiple goals, all at once. At the most basic level, getting kids involved adds more immediate friends to the roster - people who will volunteer, give advice on your programs, donate (yes, kids make great donors), talk with others about your mission. These are meaningful short-term goals, as kids learn firsthand about the abundance of resources each of us has to give, regardless of age.

At the next level, for every kid that gets involved, there is usually a parent that is made aware of your programs. And that adds yet another prospective adult friend to your ranks.

At an even higher level, getting kids involved in your organization's cause can ignite a passion for your mission at an early enough age that those children can become friends for life. Whether these growing children stay in your geographic area as adults, or move across the world, you will have opened their minds to the cause you believe in and helped show them ways of making their world a better place, wherever they land. What an amazing gift to give to these young friends!

Lastly, never forget the incredible gift all our communities receive when organizations consciously engage kids directly in the work of planning, goal setting, program creation and implementation. If our programs are going to be relevant not just today, but 5 and 10 years from now, ignoring the wisdom of young people disregards a critical source of expertise for any organization's mission - from arts to animal shelter to education to human services. Further, if your organization's mission is in any way related to youth issues, failure to deeply engage young people in your programs may just be downright irresponsible!

Strategies in this section include:

Asking Schools for Help

The first year we targeted schools to help with the Diaper Drive, we had no idea how that effort would turn into one of our most successful FriendRaising campaigns. Within a few short years, schools were providing as many as one quarter the total diapers collected during the whole Diaper Drive! More importantly, we were creating friendships that grew as the children grew. Our direct experience of working with schools taught us how much we all have to learn.

What Do Schools Have To Do With Our Program?

Depending on the nature of your organization, there are a variety of reasons to connect with kids in schools - from preschoolers up through high school. For some programs, connecting with kids in school is part of your mission. Others may generate interest through sponsorship and other means. Still for others, collections of goods and even cash donations can happen in the schools.

But more importantly, schools are where kids learn. And everything about learning has to do with your organization, regardless of your mission.

What is the Goal of this Strategy?

The goal of working with school kids will depend on your organization, but for all

	STRATEGY	Asking Schools for Help
	#57	**Your Mission at School**
	STRATEGY	Asking Schools for Help
	#58	**Getting Advice**
	STRATEGY	Asking Schools for Help
	#59	**Sponsoring School Activities**
	STRATEGY	Asking Schools for Help
	#60	**Collect Goods**
	STRATEGY	Asking Schools for Help
	#61	**Collect Pennies**
	STRATEGY	Asking Schools for Help
	#62	**Benefit from School Events**
	STRATEGY	Asking Schools for Help
	#63	**Public Speaking**

organizations, the goal will be engagement in its truest form. If we involve young people in the things that are important to their future, from our mission work to the value of giving back, and also teach them to see the many resources they do have to share, we have invested in a better future for the communities we serve.

But also keep in mind the other side of the coin - we can learn from kids as much as we teach. The goal, therefore, becomes bigger than just a friendship with your individual organization. The goal becomes as big as the whole issue of community engagement. And many teachers and Parent Teacher Organizations are happy to add this level of engagement to the work they do with their kids.

Who Will We Target with These Strategies?

Looking at your Life List, the target for these strategies will be anyone with kids in school, including your own kids, as well as teachers or others who work in the school system.

How to Involve Schools In Your Mission

The first step in working with schools will be to use some of the strategies in the previous sections of this book to bring those individuals with kids in schools - or those who work in the schools - into your organization's family. Then you and your friend can work together (or your friend can work with the Executive Director or other staff) to introduce the organization to the appropriate person at the school. Sometimes that is the principal, sometimes the head of the PTO, sometimes the head of the Student Council. Work with those individuals to introduce your mission, and to brainstorm ways their school's kids might help.

As you read through the following activities, be sure to jot down any additional ideas that come to mind, to see if there is a fit with the schools in your area.

Important Note:

Before you contact anyone or ask for anything related to this section's activities, understand the following:

Schools have their own mission - one that no one will argue is critically important to the future of our communities. With the rapid increase in testing demands, schools are struggling just to find time to teach. As you approach school representatives, be a true friend - be respectful and considerate of the fact that schools have a tough time simply doing the job they are expected to do. Plan to work around their needs. As you approach teachers and parents with your ideas, that consideration will go a long way to creating the long term relationship you hope to build.

STRATEGY #57 | Bringing Mission-Focused Activities to School

There are many social service organizations whose missions focus on children. Child abuse (treatment and prevention), teen pregnancy (prevention and direct services), AIDS - the list goes on. If your organization is looking to get a program exposed directly to kids, connecting with parents and teachers who are already part of the school system is a great way to begin.

However there are also organizations whose missions are not directly about "youth" - the arts, environment, animal rights, etc. - where educating kids certainly furthers your mission. And connecting with parents and teachers is a great way to introduce these programs into one school at a time.

STRATEGY #58 | Getting Advice

Students of all ages, as well as their parents and teachers, are great resources for getting advice to make your programs more effective. These caring community members are an untapped group of advisors, with tremendous knowledge and expertise in diverse areas - from teen pregnancy and substance abuse to community arts programs and historic preservation.

As you connect with students, teachers and parents, use the Community Sleuthing and Focus Group approaches in Strategies #10 and #24 to determine how your programs can be even more effective to meet your communities needs and aspirations. Once you have involved kids at this level, if you find you want more direct and ongoing connection with their wisdom and experience, work with those very kids to determine the best ways to ensure young people are woven into your organization's fabric.

Remember, asking individuals for advice is a way of showing them the respect you have for their wisdom, their experience, their knowledge. Kids so often feel as if their wisdom and experience are discounted (and often they are) - that they are "just kids." By creating real communication about your programs, and following up to further involve young people in those issues, you are creating real friendships - real engagement.

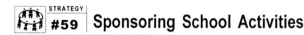
 ## STRATEGY #59 | Sponsoring School Activities

As we discussed in Strategy #56, sponsorship is not a donation; it is the providing of goods or services (including cash, but not necessarily) in exchange for publicity. Unlike your intent in that previous strategy, however, this strategy is not about asking a school to sponsor your organization. This strategy is about your organization sponsoring the school!

"Sponsorship" does not have to mean an exchange of money. Sponsorship can mean that your organization provides any sort of support - often in-kind support - in exchange for publicity. And if your organization will receive not only publicity, but the opportunity to further its mission with school-aged kids at the same time, you can see why sponsorship of these types of efforts is a great way to build solid friendships.

For-profit companies clearly see the value of this effort when it comes to schools. Many of the marquee signs we see outside local schools these days have the logo of a fast-food restaurant at the bottom, to thank the business that paid for the sign.

Because "sponsorship" does not necessarily require a donation of money, nonprofit organizations can easily be sponsors of something the school wants to do. For example, your environmental group, "Friends of My Town," could sponsor the Earth Day Fair a school is already doing. Friends of My Town might provide judges for their competition, a speaker for the event, literature, T-shirts - whatever makes sense for the organization and for the event.

In exchange for what Friends of My Town will be doing for the school, all publicity for the event would say, "Sponsored in part by Friends of My Town." Friends of My Town could do a press release and local radio/tv talk shows about the collaboration with the school, and why they are helping to sponsor the event. And copies of any press clippings could be included in future Friends of My Town funding requests, as proof of their commitment to the broader community and their efforts towards collaboration.

Now before you say, "We would have given them those T-shirts and judges anyway - we don't need all that publicity!", the answer is that yes, you may have. But there are two reasons to indeed take the publicity that is available.

The first reason is simple - it's publicity! Almost every organization wishes it had more publicity, and this is mission-driven publicity - the best kind.

Secondly, though, this publicity shows the community your level of engagement with real people doing real things - your mission in practice

STRATEGY #60 | Collect Goods

If your organization could use food, blankets, socks, school supplies - anything you provide as part of your mission - school kids are often great missionaries, not only collecting those goods, but spreading the message of why you need them.

By collecting goods, kids learn of the need in a tangible and visceral way, and they carry that understanding with them as they grow up. Collecting goods by connecting up with area schools, even just one classroom at a time, will spread both your mission to provide those goods, and your mission to raise awareness of the reasons behind the need for those goods.

 **STRATEGY #61** | ## Collect Pennies

Depending on your organization, penny jars are a great way for school kids to learn a variety of lessons about giving back. Pennies are the great leveler - the lowest income of low income kids can put a penny into the jar and feel that they, too, have contributed. And anyone who has put her change in a jar each night knows how quickly those coins add up!

Again, this is a way all kids can learn that everyone has resources that are important to making their community a better place to live

STRATEGY #62 | ## Benefiting From School Events

Depending on the organization and depending on the event, it is possible to receive joint publicity AND some donations by having a school event benefit your organization. For example, your local high school drama department might be pleased to have a charitable tie-in for their upcoming play, as it could give them a way to promote the play in the local newspaper (and therefore potentially increase attendance).

The event that benefits your organization does not have to be public. A middle school dance (or the proceeds from snacks sold at the dance) could benefit your cause as well. One year a group of elementary school students sold pickles at lunchtime to benefit the Diaper Bank!

STRATEGY #63 | ## Public Speaking

Finally, schools offer great opportunities for sharing your mission through public speaking. Whether you are speaking to an individual high school class, the PTA, or the whole elementary school gathered cross-legged on the floor of the cafeteria, the ability to share your mission with kids of all ages is a powerful way to engage lifelong friends.

What is the Role of the Board Member in this Strategy?

The role of the Board Member for this strategy is simple. If you have children in school yourself, make the connections between your child's teacher or principal and determine if there might be a fit with your organization.

If you have no kids in school, talk with friends who are involved with the schools (parents or teachers), and determine if any of these activities is potentially a fit for their school. If there is a flicker of interest, connect your friend with the Executive Director, and the two of them will quickly be able to determine how to proceed.

If there is no fit, you will have introduced one more of your friends to the organization, which is always a good thing!

AT THE DIAPER BANK

The Diaper Bank's first school campaign was almost an afterthought. Learning that a number of schools were already collecting diapers during our annual campaign, we held a party for them in the back parking lot of our office. With so few schools, it was easy to convince some locally-owned fast food restaurants to provide pizza and slushies for all the kids.

Since then, the School Drive has become a mainstay of the Diaper Bank's collection efforts. Part of that effort focuses on contests to raise the most diapers, or to raise them in the most creative ways. And part of it focuses on the bigger picture, raising awareness about the real issues of poverty and crisis.

Participation in the contests varies. Some schools just want to collect diapers without competing for prizes. Those who do participate in the contests, however, often compete with a vengeance. We provide prizes to the school that collects the most diapers; to the school that collects the most diapers per student (to ensure even a small school can win); and to the "School with the Most Heart."

As a result, we have had as many as 60 schools participating in the Diaper Drive, with the number ever-increasing.

One year, Tucson Hebrew Academy's 6th grade class posed this challenge: "If our class doesn't raise the most diapers, we will all dress like babies." The 6th grade did raise the most diapers, and to celebrate, they all wore baby clothes anyway. When the local NBC news affiliate showed up to interview and film these incredible kids, it made for quite a story!

At Borton Elementary, a tiny school that only goes as high as 2nd grade, the teachers turned their diaper collections into an opportunity to teach math. The kids charted their progress all around the hallways, learning to use graphs and hash marks and all different ways of counting to tally those diapers.

Because middle school is where "cool" becomes gospel, some kids think it is extremely **un**cool to collect diapers. So Ms. Wilson's 7th grade social studies class at Booth-Fickett Magnet School chose instead to talk about the issue of how poverty can exist in a wealthy country like the U.S. Following that discussion, Ms. Wilson's class collected over $200 in change for the Diaper Bank. She told us if she forgot to pass the jar each day, the kids were vocal in reminding her. While mostly they just added the change in their pockets, a number of kids emptied their piggy banks, telling their teacher they could not bear the thought of a mom being unable to diaper her baby.

As for the thought that a school must be located in a wealthy part of town to be able to help out, our experience proves what fundraisers have known for years - those with the least often give the most. One year, the "School with the Most Heart" was located on a nearby Indian Reservation, where the kids collected diapers with a passion. Another year, teachers at the lowest income school in our very large school district initiated a penny drive, prohibiting anything larger than a penny, so every child could participate equally - raising over $200 in the process. The teachers in these schools acknowledge that many of their families are actually the recipients of our diapers. They feel it is therefore even more important that the kids learn the sense of pride and accomplishment that comes from understanding that they do indeed have many gifts and resources to share.

And that gets to the heart of what friendship is about, and why building friendships between school-aged kids and your organization is so important. In the Diaper Drive's early years, no self-respecting middle or high school kid would consider collecting for the Diaper Drive. But after all these years, Tucson's kids have been collecting diapers since they were in 1st Grade. There is no longer any shame in collecting diapers at any age - only excitement about helping those in need.

Asking Kids for Help Outside of School

For volunteers, for collecting diapers, for getting the word out - the Diaper Bank has been blessed with the support of Girl Scouts and Boy Scouts and church youth groups and any kind of youth organization you could imagine.

What Do Scouts and Soccer Teams Have to Do With Your Organization?

Kids' organizations offer a unique way to tap into the natural desire on the part of kids to help other people. While organizations such as scout troops or congregation youth groups are often looking for ways to teach kids about giving back, soccer and basketball teams gather large groups of kids and parents together and can also be a great venue for finding help and building friendships.

	STRATEGY	Asking Kids for Help Outside of School
	#64	**Volunteer Groups**
	STRATEGY	Asking Kids for Help Outside of School
	#65	**Remember the Parents**
	STRATEGY	Asking Kids for Help Outside of School
	#66	**A-thons**
	STRATEGY	Asking Kids for Help Outside of School
	#67	**Program Advice**

What is the Goal of this Strategy?

The goals for this strategy are the same as the goals for all the other strategies involving kids. The most obvious one is to merely add additional new friends to your roster, as well as adding a new group who can help with the things your organization needs, not to mention the side benefit - the friendships formed with their parents. But the more important goal is to show kids how much they have to give, even (and especially) at their age.

Who Should We Include in this Strategy?

These strategies will apply to the people on your Life List who have children in extra-curricular activities, or who have kids in school, including your own.

How to Get Kids' Groups Involved

Depending on the nature of your organization, there are a number of ways to get groups of kids involved. The following are just a start.

 **Volunteer Groups**

If your organization has a task that requires physical labor, a group of kids can often fit the bill perfectly. A back lot that needs to be cleared of trash? A mailing that needs to be folded and sent? These are great tasks for kids to perform.

Start the activity by gathering the kids (and their parents) around and giving them a brief (3 minutes) explanation of what your organization does, and why the work they are about to do is so important to your mission. Tell them a story - stories go farther faster than merely talking about what you do. If they are to grow to become true philanthropists, it is important that they not only do the work, but understand why they are doing the work.

When the work is done, gather the group for a photo - not before, when they are clean and neat, but after, when they are dirty and tired and feeling goofy. When you send the group leader his/her thank you note, include enough 4"x6" copies of that photo for each person in the photo. You might even include an 8"x10" photo for the whole organization, to go into their scrap book or on the wall of their meeting place.

If this is an activity you will be doing more than once, consider having a graphic designer create a customized digital frame for your photos, as described on page 81.

STRATEGY #65 | Remember the Parents

Depending on the age of the kids involved in these activities, frequently you will have just as many parents present as children. This is a great way to connect with those individuals. Ask parents to sign in, providing their contact information, so you can send thank you notes and announcements of other volunteer activities, etc. Then don't forget to send those notes, along with the photo!

STRATEGY #66 | A-thons

Walk-a-thons. Fun runs. Spell-a-thons. If your organization relies on these types of events for revenue, kids' clubs are great for getting teams of participants. Ask your friends if their children's groups would be interested in signing up to participate.

STRATEGY #67 | Program Advice

This is mentioned in the section on schools, but it is so important, it bears repeating.

Who better to aks about kids becoming addicted to drugs than the kids themselves? Who better to help guide programs that educate families about the power of the arts, than the families themselves? If any part of your program touches the lives of kids, doesn't it make sense to involved kids integrally in the process of developing and improving the effectiveness of those programs?

Use the Community Sleuthing and Focus Group approaches found in Strategies #10 and #24 to help guide this process, as well as the Interactive Coffee technique in Strategy #12. This may be the start of an ongoing program to involve this valuable resource - the young people in our communities - in the programs that will affect their lives.

What is the Role of the Board Member in this Strategy?

The role of Board Members in this activity is simple - call friends and ask if their kids would be willing to help out. Have information ready to provide to your friend, as it is likely he/she will not be the one to make the final decision - that will likely fall to the scout leader, soccer coach, etc. Once your friend gets the ok, the appropriate staff or volunteer at your organization can determine the best way to coordinate this effort. And remember, if your friends are not already friends of the organization's mission, the first step will be ensuring they are properly introduced and brought into the family.

AT THE DIAPER BANK

Every year during December Diaper Drive, hundreds of thousands of diapers arrive at the warehouse. Those diapers need to be sorted by size, counted into inventory, then put away. That task is handled every year by hosting a Sorting Party. (See Strategies #21 - 23)

And that is when the Boy Scouts Catalina Council Troop 777 comes to the rescue.

As we do with every volunteer event, we start the day by gathering the volunteers to hear the story of why those diapers are important - that it is not just about the Diapers, but about the people whose lives are so vulnerable, that these diapers make the difference between a healthy, safe existence, or one of abuse, neglect, disease.

And then we line out the troops and send them to work. Within hours, the Boy Scouts sort and count so many diapers that what might otherwise be a week's worth of work is done in a few hours. (We also benefit from the pair of scouts who have been known to don clown costumes and stand on the street corner, leading attendees to the event!)

Most of the kids remember a fun event, working alongside their parents and siblings (we always encourage kids to bring friends). That makes our event an easy sell the following year. But the ripples go farther than just that.

The sister of one of the scouts in Troop 777 took what she learned that day, and had her school do a diaper drive. Parents often send a donation, or tell others about the work we are doing.

At the end of the day, our work is done, our mission is spread, and the Boy Scouts have done a great community service project. But more than that, we have made tons of friends - friends who will get a thank you and a photo, who will be invited to events, and who will be back next year to sort more diapers. The Diaper Bank, the Boy Scouts and the community are all better for that wonderful friendship.

Brainstorm Sheet: _____

❖ Asking Kids for Help

What areas of connection are there between your organization's mission and area school kids? _____

1.) _____

2.) _____

3.) _____

4.) _____

5.) _____

6.) _____

Are there ways your programs could increase their effectiveness by getting advice and involvement from kids? What could you learn from them? What could you ask?

_____

1.) _____

2.) _____

3.) _____

4.) _____

5.) _____

6.) _____

List activities at your organization that could be helped by an eager group of kids.

_____

1.) _____

2.) _____

3.) _____

4.) _____

5.) _____

6.) _____

❖ ASKING CONGREGATIONS FOR HELP

When we look back over more than 10 years of collecting diapers, it is hard for us to find a religious denomination that has not had a hand in the Diaper Bank's ability to help those who need it. From that experience, we have learned the secret formula for working with congregations. The secret is simple: *There is no formula*. Each congregation has helped in a way that has made sense for them. Each has suggested a different contact person - from the head of the youth group to the pastor himself. Each has suggested a different way to help.

From those efforts, we have learned two important lessons about asking congregations for help. First, for many causes - and not just human service causes - places of worship are a wonderful place to engage with friends of your mission. While we tend to immediately think of faith organizations supporting human services, in reality, arts and the environment and other organizations have just as much to gain by including congregations in their thinking.

Second, though, we learned that every faith is different. Every denomination within each of those faiths is different. And every congregation within each of those denominations is different. If working with congregations will be part of your focus (and we believe it should be), it will require that you acknowledge, before you begin, that assuming all congregations are the same is much like assuming all families are the same.

While it takes time and attention to work with congregations, the rewards for your community are worth it. The reason for that is simple - places of worship are about coming together in a spirit of finding the common goodness in all of us. And each of our nonprofit organizations is about the very same thing.

Asking Congregations for Help

Places of worship have helped the Diaper Bank since the first days of our first Diaper Drive. They have collected diapers, shared their wisdom, provided speaking opportunities, given cash donations, volunteered - and some have even distributed diapers to those in need. If there is any group worth engaging as true friends, it is congregations.

What Do Congregations Have to Do with Our Program?

There is almost nothing your organization needs, from advice on programs to volunteers to in-kind donations to raising money, that congregations cannot provide. Because "faith" is about our whole lives, congregations are a wonderful place for engaging with people who are passionate about making life better.

We have become used to thinking of "faith-based service organizations" as primarily addressing the physical human con-

STRATEGY	Asking Congregations for Help
#68	**Speaking Opportunities**

STRATEGY	Asking Congregations for Help
#69	**Volunteers**

STRATEGY	Asking Congregations for Help
#70	**Donation of Goods or Cash**

STRATEGY	Asking Congregations for Help
#71	**Program Advice**

STRATEGY	Asking Congregations for Help
#72	**The "Church Bulletin"**

STRATEGY	Asking Congregations for Help
#73	**Congregation Leadership**

dition. And while the Diaper Bank certainly falls into that category, we have also found interest among congregations for issues that go beyond the human service arena.

If the arts are simply an expression of the human spirit, what better place to talk about that than in a place that celebrates what is best in all of us? If part of faith includes caring for the earth and the creatures on this earth, what better place to talk about environmental issues than with those who care about our world in such a way? History, education, human rights, international relations - there is something in each of these issues that touches the soul.

And that makes congregations a wonderful place for engaging friends with your mission.

What is the Goal of this Strategy?

The goal of this strategy will depend on each congregation and each person you contact, as well as the goals of your organization itself. After getting to know individuals from congregations where there is a fit, the goals could be the goals of any one of the efforts described in this book, and certainly the goals of your Community Engagement Plan. Therefore, the most important goal will be a high level of engagement, to bring to light those things with which it make most sense for that particular congregation to help.

Who Will We Target for this Strategy?

For this strategy, your Board Members will connect with any of the individuals on their Life Lists who are involved with their congregations. Because every congregation is different, the best introduction to each individual congregation will be someone who is already on the "inside" - someone who can tell you how decisions are made at that congregation, and can tell you who is in charge of various aspects of those decisions.

In addition, this person will likely have some familiarity with some of the groups that may be active at that congregation. Those groups will vary, from the whole congregation to kids Sunday School classes, from youth groups to women's auxiliaries, from study / discussion groups to language classes, and etc.

The first step will be to use some of the strategies in the previous sections of this book to bring that new friend - your link to that congregation - into your organization's family. Once you have done that, you and your new friend can work together to determine what approaches will make sense for his/her particular congregation.

The next step from there will be to have your friend introduce you to whoever is appropriate for your organization to work with at that congregation.

You can see that the process of engaging with congregations can take some time, as it is often not a direct link, but many links that must be made before you find the right fit for a particular congregation. After your friend, the next person you meet with may be the Men's Prayer Group leader, or the principal of the Hebrew School, or the Imam. Working with congregations is a slow getting-to-know-you process, as this is not a place of business, where things must happen quickly, and it is not a school, where there is little time for anything that is not direct and to the point. A place of worship is a place where the soul rests. And that means you may want to take a breath and slow down as you work to engage this group of potential friends.

How to Get Congregations Involved

We have mentioned that there are almost as many ways congregations can help your mission as there are congregations. The following are just a few ideas. As you go through this book, looking at strategies for other groups, your thinking may spark on additional ways a particular congregation can become an integral part of your organization's work. And as always, engage friends from those congregations to help brainstorm additional ways their groups can share what they have to offer.

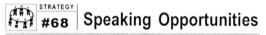 **STRATEGY #68 Speaking Opportunities**

Depending on the size of the congregation, and the number of sub-groups within that congregation, we have seen a single congregation provide 5 or 6 different speaking opportunities, with entirely different groups! The youth group, the community outreach group, the men's group, the women's group, the study group, the Executive Board - particularly in large congregations, there are sometimes more meetings going on than one would ever think possible!

Unlike other speaking engagements, where it is often less-than-appropriate to directly ask for things like donations and volunteers, often congregations are more amenable to being asked for such assistance. Unlike a Civitan or Rotary group, where speakers may be cautioned not to ask for donations, congregation-related groups are often excited to be able to immediately dig in and help. And while an effective speech still would not focus on such requests, be prepared to address some of your wish list items from Strategy #3 when you finish your talk, as one of the first questions may just be, "How can we help?"

 **STRATEGY #69 Volunteers**

If you have a volunteer activity, congregations are often a great source for volunteers. Use the volunteer activity as you would in Strategies #21 - 23, following up with photos and thank you's. If you can make that volunteer activity fun and engaging, congregation volunteers are often the ones to come back again and again.

Friend Raising

STRATEGY #70 | Donations of Goods or Cash

Some congregation-related groups look for projects where they can collect goods or cash for an organization. Some adopt one organization to help throughout the year; others rotate their support to a different group each month; while still others save their giving for holiday time. Again, each congregation will have a different approach to these collections.

STRATEGY #71 | Program Advice

Faith-related groups gather not because they are required to be there, but because they want to be there, to make life better. Given that virtually every mission of every community organization is a mission of the spirit - from caring about animals to caring about education to caring about the arts as an expression of our humanity - getting input from a group of caring individuals from a local congregation is an excellent way to engage these passionate people in your mission. Use the Community Sleuthing and Focus Group approaches in Strategies #10 and #24 to help make your programs as effective as they can be.

STRATEGY #72 | The "Church Bulletin"

Many congregations have a newsletter that goes to members of that congregation. Some are sent in the mail monthly, some are handed out as a one-page sheet every week during religious services, and some congregations have multiple newsletters, again depending on the size of the congregation.

These newsletters offer many opportunities to share your story. (For more about how to take advantage of these newsletters and bulletins, see Strategies #34 and #35.)

STRATEGY #73 | Engage with the Congregation's Spiritual Leader

As you engage with individuals active within a particular congregation, getting to know the leader in that congregation is an important part of engaging with the congregation as a whole. The point of building a relationship with that spiritual leader will not be to ask for anything, but to engage that person with the work your organization is doing - to make a friend.

As you form your organization's "Dream Team" from Strategy #40; as you look for local celebrities to speak about your cause; as you look to be connected with other religious leaders in the community - the Priest or Imam or Rabbi is someone whose friendship can be helpful to your organization in many many ways. Importantly, as you look to gain wisdom to help your programs, input from these spiritual leaders can be invaluable.

Because these individuals have dedicated their lives to making life better for others, building a relationship with people in those positions is often a friendship that is a true blessing for both your organization and that place of worship.

What is the Role of the Board Member in this Strategy?

The role of the Board Member in this strategy is to first contact any individuals on your Life List who are involved with their congregations, and to engage those people in your organization's work. Take them on a tour or to breakfast, or use any of the other strategies for making that first connection.

From there, the Board Member may wish to have an ongoing role in connecting with others at that congregation, or that task my be taken up by the organization's staff. But that initial introduction is the key, acting as the liaison between your organization and the congregations in your community.

AT THE DIAPER BANK

It is hard to overstate the support the Diaper Bank has received from congregations in our community. The following are a sampling of those efforts, but we could fill this whole book with examples.

The youth group at a local Evangelical Christian church delivers a carload of diapers to the Diaper Bank each month, while the ladies' auxiliary from a local Methodist congregation sends a $250 check a few times a year.

One young man dedicated his Bar Mitzvah project to collecting diapers, asking his guests to bring diapers for the Diaper Bank. The announcement of that effort was sent to all his family and friends, and even made the local newspaper, as this young man told anyone who would listen that he wanted to help those in need, "One tush at a time."

Every January, a group of 50+ congregations collects tens of thousands of diapers through a multi-congregation effort of the Southern Arizona Life Team.

And as for speaking engagements, congregations provide a steady stream of such opportunities. One recent example was an issues discussion group of 30 people, all of whom appeared to be 75 years old or older. The group meets after services every Sunday to discuss the critical issues facing the community. Having seen me on a local public affairs interview program (again, the value of those longer interviews is always more potent than we imagine - see Strategy #36), this group wanted to talk about the poverty issues that underlie the seemingly simple commodity of "diapers."

If your board applied the strategies in this book only to working with your community's congregations, the board would never run out of ways to engage these individuals who care passionately about your community's quality of life.

Brainstorm Sheet: _____

❖ Asking Congregations for Help

How Can Congregations Help Your Organization?

What areas of connection are there between the mission of your organization, and the life of the spirit? Does your organization connect with issues of compassion? Is your organization's mission related to stewardship? Is your mission uplifting, joyfully sharing the spirit of life? Discuss with your board the ways your mission relates to the spirit as it is understood through the various faiths and denominations in your community.

_____

_____

_____

_____

_____

_____

_____

_____

Note: As your board discusses these topics, you may find your board will want to learn more about the faiths that are present in your community. And there is no better way to engage with a congregation than to ask a representative to come talk to your organization about what connections they feel there might be between their faith and the work your organization is doing!

❖ ASKING DONORS FOR HELP

One way friends can indeed help our organizations is to donate cash.

Seen from a FriendRaising approach, however, fundraising is not an end in and of itself, but a part of something bigger. And while the money goals will only be a small part of your overall community engagement goals, you may find you will raise more money with this approach than you have with traditional money-as-the-goal approaches.

Because the goal is friendship in all its facets, your goal in this section will not be to ask friends for money. The goal will be to invite the people your organization has thus far considered only as "donors" to become real and true friends.

As with all the other strategies in this book, this section will provide approaches all your board would be comfortable participating in. That is because these are approaches that simply seek the assistance and guidance of a real friend.

Strategies in this section include:

#74   Making Change

#75 - #76   Using Your Direct Mail Campaign to Engage Donors as Friends

#77   Inviting Your Large Donors to Become Friends

STRATEGY

#74 | Making Change

The Diaper Bank has collected hundreds of dollars the donors did not think of as donations - hundreds of dollars that were barely noticed by those donors. And we accomplished that by asking Board Members to empty their change at board meetings.

Watching that change add up, we quickly realized the power of using this approach beyond just our board. We also realized there were lessons to learn beyond just money when we asked folks to help by collecting change.

What Is Collecting Change?

If you have ever been the type to empty your change into a jar when you get home at night, you will know the following to be true:

1) Change adds up quickly.

2) Once you have emptied it from your pocket, you do not miss it.

This strategy is therefore to simply ask folks to save their change for your organization.

What is the Goal of this Strategy?

The goal for this strategy is cash, but it is also more than that.

The money part is easy to understand. Asking friends to collect their change for your organization is perhaps the least intimidating way to ask for cash donations.

We worked with a group whose Board Members emptied their change at every meeting, and every month deposited $80 in the bank. That is almost $1,000 a year, just by dumping out their change at every board and committee meeting. The organization's whole budget was $100,000. They made up 1% of their budget by emptying their change at meetings!

But the more complex part has to do with seeing how much each of us has to share. At almost every income level, this strategy can be effective in showing how important each contribution is to the whole.

Who Will This Strategy Target?

The first target for this strategy will be your own board. From there, this is an easy strategy to suggest to those on your Life List who are members of clubs or congregations, or any other group that gathers regularly. It is also something you can ask anyone from your Life List to do on their own, at home.

How to Collect Change

Coins add up. If every Board Member asked just one person to get members of her book club, softball league, church choir, or even her family to save their change, imagine how those pennies will start to add up! This strategy gives you the opportunity to talk to your friend(s) about your cause, to share why the mission is so important to you that even their spare change matters.

And don't forget to ask spouses and friends to save their own change. Once they are giving their change on a regular basis, it is a simple step to ask them to spread that effort to their own friends - through their bowling leagues, their birdwatching groups, their garden clubs.

What is the Role of the Board Member in this Strategy?

The role of the Board Member in this particular activity will be to think of as many places as possible where change can be collected to benefit the organization. And at the very least, it is the role of the Board Member to empty his/her change and save it to give to your organization.

DO THE MATH

If your board has 10 Board Members, and they each have a dollar in their pockets during your board meeting, that is $10 per meeting that can go to your organization. After a year of board meetings, that is $120 dollars your board will have donated without noticing it was gone!

In truth, though, the money adds up faster than that. When the Diaper Bank board was a tiny start-up board of only 5 or 6 Board Members, after 3 meetings we had collected $100. Now at every meeting, the presence of our baby bottle bank immediately tells us to empty our pockets. (Diaper Bank Board Members are also expected to bring diapers to every meeting - to remind us all of how expensive these items are, and how hard it is for low income families to afford them.)

In another case, we were working with a client who decided that wherever members of the board gathered - whether it was for a board meeting or committee meeting - their "blue jar" would always be there. They voted that the contents of the jar would go into a separate account, to cover things like flowers for a birthday or a funeral - the kinds of things the board felt they would prefer not to dip into the general fund to provide.

At this organization's annual planning session, they passed the blue jar early in the day. Then they got to work, wrangling not only with big issues, but also with some of the smaller obstacles that had fallen through the cracks.

During lunch, the Board President counted the change in the blue jar, announcing the total: $80 from just that one meeting! And the board immediately voted to use that money to address one of the issues the staff had identified just that morning as having fallen through the cracks.

The effect of that effort went beyond just the money. It allowed the staff to see that the board was serious about addressing the concerns they had raised. And it allowed the board to immediately see the impact of even these tiny gifts.

While $80 and $100 certainly is not a lot of money, it is larger than the $25 checks organizations often receive in their direct mail campaigns. And unlike the direct mail campaign, that $100 comes with zero expense. If someone offered to write you a check right now for that amount, you would be happy to take it, regardless of how large your organization is!

Those small donations add up, and the beautiful thing is that this is money no one will think twice about giving. Collecting change is therefore not only "easy money"; it is a way to share publicly in a small but significant way.

Using Your Direct Mail Campaign to Engage Donors as Friends

Because the Diaper Bank started as Dimitri and my little philanthropic effort, those first few years, we never asked anyone for financial assistance. After all, this was our giving back. We just didn't feel right asking others to do any more than give diapers.

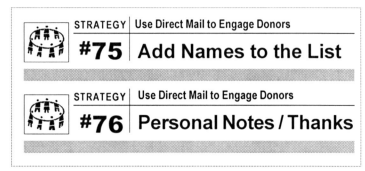

What we did want to do, however, was crow a bit! During our first Diaper Drive, we collected 20,000 diapers with virtually no planning. Jumping to Year 4, we brought in almost 175,000.

Then in Year 5, we tried something different. When we wrote our annual Help 4 NonProfits holiday newsletter, we not only chronicled our consulting adventures, but our diaper adventures as well. And on every letter, we wrote a personal note to the recipient, asking them to bring in diapers, to see if we could beat the prior year's collections.

What we never expected from that note was that our friends started to send us money. Talk about being unprepared! Being a for-profit company simply doing something charitable, we did not even have a way to handle those funds!

And while we quickly figured out how to legally address the issues surrounding those donations, we just as quickly realized the power of asking people we knew for help with something we cared about. We had asked for diapers. And while many brought us diapers, many also sent us dollars. That newsy letter about our adventures brought in $10,000 that we used to make our first bulk purchase of 100,000 diapers.

In looking back, we know now that what we did is classic direct mail fundraising. But we also know why it works. It is just as much about asking for money as it is about engaging with a friend.

What Does Direct Mail Have to Do with Engaging Friends?

One of the easiest and most effective ways to raise money is through a direct mail campaign. Most organizations do at least some direct mail, even if they do not think of it as that. Whether your organization has a full-blown direct mail effort, or you send just a one-page newsy letter at holiday time, this effort could be helping you to do more than just raise money. It could be helping you connect with new friends, and it could be helping you turn some of your existing donors into real friends.

There are tons of books and other resources about creating effective direct mail campaigns from the perspective of fundraising. (See the AfterWords for some suggestions.) This workbook, however, is specifically about boards and raising *friends*, not funds. Therefore, this strategy will focus on the role Board Members can play in broadening the results you anticipate from your Direct Mail efforts, by further engaging your friends.

What is the Goal of this Effort?

The goal of this effort is to increase the results of your existing direct mail campaign in two ways. The first is to increase the number of gifts you receive from your Direct Mail efforts. In addition, though, the longer term goal is to expand those results beyond just money, taking the opportunity to more deeply engage your existing donors in the work your organization is doing - inviting them to become real friends.

Who Should We Target for this Strategy?

This strategy should include everyone on your Life List. Yes, everyone! It will also include anyone you have met through other strategies in this book, including your Community Sleuthing and other efforts.

How Board Members Can Use Your Direct Mail Campaign to Engage Friends

 STRATEGY #75 Add Names to the Mailing List

For each individual on your Life List, including those you have met through the activities in this book, gather addresses and contact information (email addresses, too). Add those individuals to your organization's mailing list. Any newsletters and direct mail pieces the organization regularly sends should now go to those individuals as well.

STRATEGY #76 Writing Personal Notes and Thanks You's to Engage Your Friends

Statistically, the return on a mailing increases if the recipient receives a personal request to give from someone he/she knows. Therefore, the more often your Board Members can go through your direct mail appeals, writing a personal note to the individuals they know and re-connecting those individuals with the organization's mission, the more your organization will be able to enhance its fundraising efforts.

The thing about this strategy that appeals to many Board Members from that fundraising perspective is a) direct mail giving does not usually ask for huge amounts of money, and b) it is not face-to-face. Given that combination, most Board Members will not object to writing a note asking their friends to help however they can.

From a FriendRaising perspective, however, adding that personal note gives you the opportunity to more deeply engage those who have, to date, only written checks but not become real friends.

Therefore, have your board go through the mailing list each time your organization does a mailing, looking for the people they know. And have them write a *short* personal note to each of those people.

Those notes will use just one or two short lines to tell friends that:
- These issues are special to you
- Any amount they give will be put to good use and be appreciated
- You would love to give them a tour if they are interested (or take them for coffee and tell them more, etc.)

That's it.

This short note will perform multiple functions in engaging those friends. Yes, it will gently ask for money, which is always helpful. But it will also invite the recipient to become a friend in addition to becoming a donor, by asking them to think about the organization's work, and inviting them to learn more. Once you have made that initial invitation, it is far easier to follow up, to engage them with some of the other activities listed in this book.

The Thank You

The last step in this process applies to those who respond to your note by giving a gift. That friend will have opened the door for you to begin to engage that friendship with the organization. Call to thank your friend personally, and invite him for coffee, or to take a tour, or any of the other FriendRaising strategies in Part 2.

You can see how what was formerly an approach intended only to increase dollars can now become a tool for using **fund**raising to raise friends. By writing the note on the letter, you have initiated the relationship. By responding to their gift with an invitation to real engagement, you will be moving your friends from the status of "donor" to the status of "friend."

What is the Role of the Board Member in this Strategy?

The role of the Board Member in this strategy is simple and direct: provide names of friends to send the appeal, and write notes on each of those appeal letters. If your friend responds with a donation, write a personal thank-you note yourself, inviting him/her to learn more. And lastly, follow up with those who do respond, to determine their interest in learning more.

AT THE DIAPER BANK

In the beginning, the Diaper Bank's initial mailing list was a combination of the Help 4 NonProfits contact list, and each of our personal holiday card lists. With clients and friends all over the globe, after all these years we still have Diaper Bank donors from those initial lists - folks who may have been a client many years back, but have since become Diaper Bank supporters in their own right.

The key ingredient in the success of these campaigns has always been the personal note, followed up with a Thank You call.

Why go to the trouble? Two reasons.

First, the financial results are phenomenal. One year, we were considering purging the list of those who had never given. After all, these individuals had not started as "interested donors" - they started as our personal holiday card list!

Before we hit the delete key, though, we decided to try one last time. When we did our annual mailing, each of those individuals received a special note, telling them how critical their gift would be in helping those who need help the most - our community's babies, elderly and disabled. And for the first time, 30% of that list sent checks.

The more lasting reason it was worth writing those notes, however, was that it allowed us to call each person who gave, to thank them for their gift, and to talk with them about the work the Diaper Bank was doing. A number of those people came for a tour. And all these years later, many are still friends of the Diaper Bank's efforts - volunteering and helping in many ways.

Combining a personalized list with a personal note, and then following it all up with a Thank You call that invites real engagement, has value that cannot be over-emphasized. Yes, it is the easiest and least intimidating way to help raise money for your organization's mission. But it is also the road to connecting at the level of a real friend.

STRATEGY
#77 Inviting Your Large Donors to Become Friends

Until this past year, the Diaper Bank's entire budget has been around $100,000. To us, a large donor has been one who gives $500 to $1,000 annually. By turning those donors into friends, the results have been immeasurable, from finding great volunteers and Board Members to receiving incredible wisdom, to yes, increasing the size and frequency of their cash gifts.

What is this Strategy?
In every organization, the donor list can be segmented into "small" donors and "large" donors. I put those 2 words in quotation marks, because "small" and "large" are in the eye of the beholder. If your organization's total budget is $100,000, you might be thrilled to have a handful of major ongoing supporters who annually provide checks of $1,000 apiece. For a large university or hospital, that same sized donation might not receive much special attention. Regardless of what size you consider a "large" gift, your largest donors have obviously made a commitment to the organization.

In other sections of this book, we have talked about a tendency on the part of some organizations to ignore their small cash donors and their in-kind donors. We have discussed that this is what happens when we view individuals only through the lens of money.

A related effect happens when we view our large donors only through the lens of money. We stop seeing the incredible value of their friendship in its own right, and we start using what we label as "friendship" as a means to increasing the amount of money they give us. I am not sure what word I would choose for signifying "Acting like my friend because you want my money," but that word would not be "friendship". Whatever one might call that, and however one might feel about it, at the practical level it discounts what any donor has far more of than money - the capacity to share all the gifts one would share with a real friend.

When we turn our "donors" into real friends, the results are often astounding. Yes, as any fundraising expert will tell you, there is a good likelihood you will increase the size and/or frequency of their cash gifts. But you will also gain great volunteers, great cheerleaders, great introducers, great policy advocates - the same benefits you will receive from engaging all your organization's other friends.

What is the Goal of This Strategy?
The goal of this strategy is to turn your largest donors into friends, to increase their level of engagement with all the work your organization is doing in the community. The goals are therefore all the benefits of friendship that have been discussed throughout this book.

Who Will We Contact for This Strategy?
The target for this strategy are those of your existing donors who regularly give over a certain level, to be determined by analyzing your current donations.

As you look through your donor list, you will find there are a few individual donors who have given more than anyone else. If, for example, most of your gifts are in the $50-$100 range, but one or two donors give $1,000 per year, perhaps in two $500 checks - those are the gifts that stand out.

Using that list of donors, segment the list by size of gift. For this strategy, you will include anyone who has given a gift that is 25% or more of your largest gift amount, up to and including those who are currently giving at that "largest gift" amount. (As an example, if your largest gift is $1,000, your list will include anyone giving at $250 or more.) If a donor is already giving at that level *without* any degree of additional engagement, it is likely they are prime candidates to become true friends - they are already showing they care, even before you have really asked!

How to Engage Large Donors to Become Friends

In this strategy, you will contact the people on the list you created, to invite each one for a tour. You will then follow up to be sure they continue to be engaged with the work you are doing.

When you are inviting them, let them know your board thinks it is important to provide more information to the organization's best donors. Ask them if they are familiar with the new programs you have started, or the work you are doing with this group or that - whatever is new, exciting.

And ask if they would like to come by for a tour.

For those who accept your invitation for a tour, this is your chance to begin turning that "donor" relationship into a friendship.

On the day of the tour, have the ED join you, and use the approach of Community Sleuthing (Strategy #10), to learn about the donor's interests and find out what wisdom they have to share. What is it about your organization that has made her donate up to now? Find common ground. Listen more than you talk, and ask more than you answer.

The great thing about being a Board Member in this activity is that you and the donor are peers. Board Members should share with the donor the various ways *you* are supporting the organization, including your own donation (you do not have to share how much, but you can say you donate more to this organization than to any other in town). The most important thing to tell the donor is *why* you are providing that much support. What is it about the organization that compels *you* to give your support? Have a conversation, peer to peer, donor to donor, friend of the organization to friend of the organization.

Many of your donors will be too busy for a tour. That's ok. When you call, provide them with as much information about the work you are doing as is reasonable (always asking if this is a good time to talk). And as you would have done at the end of the tour, let your friend know how much you appreciate his time, as well as his ongoing support. Let him know you will be keeping him posted on whatever is new and exciting at the organization.

Then follow up your conversation with a handwritten note. Keep making it personal, building that friendship. And next time you are making your list for Community Sleuthing, a Focus Group activity, or a Volunteer Event, make sure these friends are on the list!

At the end of the tour, find out if there are areas of interest the donor would like to be involved with. Is there a task force you have set up that can use some help? A volunteer project that could use her kids' soccer team? A connection you have been trying to make with a local power-broker, that she could help make happen? The conversation will naturally get around to these areas and more. That is what happens when we engage as real friends.

As you end your time together, let your friend know you will be keeping her posted on whatever is new and exciting at the organization, especially in those areas where she has expressed interest. If you are going to have a staff person follow up with her about a particular issue, let her know it might not be you that calls, but that someone will be giving her a call from the organization.

And whether you have taken the donor for a tour, or simply chatted by phone, make sure to follow up that contact with a personal thank you note. Include with that note something related to whatever the donor expressed interest in - perhaps statistics about the success rate of your program, or an article about a new study, or the announcement from the newspaper about something amazing your organization has just accomplished.

Show that you were listening by what you send. That is the mark of a true friend.

The side benefit, as we have noted throughout this section, is that frequently just the tour alone (and the personal attention that comes with it) is enough to increase the level of that donor's gift, or to prompt an unsolicited gift in response to your thank you note. That personal touch, acknowledging this person for what he/she is - a friend, and not simply a money machine - is a big step towards increasing their level of ongoing support.

But in truth, that extra check is just a fraction of the benefit you will receive when your donors become real friends.

Make it Easy to Track Information

It is important to track pertinent details about your tour (or phone call), to be sure you and the staff can provide appropriate follow-up information to this new friend. Keeping this information in your organization's database is a big part of that tracking.

To make that tracking task easier, you might want to create a form that helps you note each friend's interests, specific things he/she mentioned, etc. The form should assist you to remember what to send them as follow up, but it should also be something you can hand to a staff person when the tour (or phone call) is over, so the staff can be sure all that information is entered into your organization's database. It would be a shame to have all this great information existing only in the memories of the people attending the tour, or on scraps of paper stuffed in the back of your Daytimer or PDA!

Have this form ready as you make your initial call, because you cannot be sure the donor will be available for a tour, and the only time you might have with her may be on the phone.

Follow Up

The key to this strategy is that the organization follow up on whatever ideas arose during your time together. If your new friend has shared wisdom, advice, suggestions - or has offered to make a connection, or to volunteer in some other way, be sure there is follow-up regarding all you discussed.

What is the Role of the Board Member in this Strategy?

Because the Board Member and the donor are peers - both are donors and both are volunteers and friends of the organization - the role of the Board Member in this strategy is everything from making that first call, to meeting the donor, to sending the thank you and following up with notes on their mailings. While the staff can help you by providing information that might be useful as they coordinate each mailing, it will be the role of the Board Member to make and maintain that personal contact until the relationship has become one of real friendship with the organization. At that time, the ED or other staff person can take over some of the "work" aspects of maintaining that friendship.

As this effort begins to swell, and the number of large donors becomes more than the board alone can manage (wouldn't this be a nice problem to have?), a committee of donor volunteers could take on this role as well. I stress "donor volunteers," as you will want to be sure donors-turned-friends are talking to other donors, peer-to-peer, about becoming real friends as well.

AT THE DIAPER BANK

At the Diaper Bank, some of our best volunteers and advisors are our donors. And while many organizations target their volunteers in the hopes they will become donors, what we did was turn those tables, encouraging our donors to become real friends.

When it is time for us to move hundreds of thousands of diapers, we call to invite our donors. When we need advice, or a committee to move forward on a new initiative, we invite our donors. When we are looking for folks to invite to Interactive Coffees and to other events - we target those donors.

Sometimes they join us, and sometimes they don't. Those who do not are always glad to be asked, as so many organizations disregard their donors when it comes to getting the real work done.

The gold of friendship has come from those who have gotten more involved with the "doing" of the Diaper Bank. When a donor has pitched in to make his/her gifts go even further, the bond between that donor and the organization has grown immediately. The desire to proudly share our mission with others has increased, and so has their desire to volunteer next time. Eventually, one or two of those donors-turned-friends have become Board Members as well.

All that is just what happens when we stop talking about providing "opportunities for them to give," and start providing opportunities to build real friendships.

Brainstorm Sheet: _____

❖ **Asking Donors for Help**

What level of gift does your organization consider a "large gift"?

_____

_____

Which of those donors who give at that level do you know personally?

1.) _____

2.) _____

3.) _____

4.) _____

5.) _____

6.) _____

How many donors give at a level that is 25% or more of your largest gifts?

_____

_____

Which of those donors who give at that level do you know personally?

1.) _____

2.) _____

3.) _____

4.) _____

5.) _____

6.) _____

You ought not to have or to love a friend for what he will give you. If you love him for the reason that he will supply you with money or some other temporal favor, you love the gift rather than him. A friend should be loved freely for himself, and not for anything else.

St. Augustine

❖ ASKING OTHER NONPROFIT ORGANIZATIONS FOR HELP

The last group we will talk about asking for help with your mission work is a group far too few community organizations include in their thinking - other nonprofit organizations. We are so used to seeing those other organizations as competition, we rarely realize how much more of a resource they could be than a threat - if we see our goal as making the community a better place.

Strategies in this section include:

Asking Other Nonprofit Organizations for Help

Picture a nonprofit organization that considers all other nonprofits its partners, not its competition. Picture an organization that includes in discussions of fundraising and media strategies statements such as, "We need to be sure we do not do this in a way that makes other agencies think we are competing with them."

Picture an organization whose values statement includes the following:

"The best decision will be the decision that provides the best end result for the highest number of our partners, the clients they serve, the issues they address, and the future of our community."

If you can picture that, you would be picturing the Diaper Bank. Because the Diaper Bank's program is collaborative at its core (see the AfterWords for more details), other organizations working on poverty issues are all seen as partners, not competitors.

	STRATEGY	Asking Other Nonprofit Organizations for Help
	#78	**Traveling Board Meetings**
	STRATEGY	Asking Other Nonprofit Organizations for Help
	#79	**Program Discussions**
	STRATEGY	Asking Other Nonprofit Organizations for Help
	#80	**Big Picture Discussions**
	STRATEGY	Asking Other Nonprofit Organizations for Help
	#81	**A Day of Tours**
	STRATEGY	Asking Other Nonprofit Organizations for Help
	#82	**Individual Tours**

The Diaper Bank's board meets in the board rooms of those other organizations (despite having a fine conference room of its own), to get better acquainted with the missions of those other agencies, and the struggles they are facing.

At the annual kick-off of the December Diaper Drive - a live radio broadcast from the park, attended by hundreds of supporters, with tremendous media coverage - all the Diaper Bank's partner agencies are invited to share the spotlight, to display information about their agencies, and to be interviewed on the radio.

The Diaper Bank knows its mission is the mission of all those otherwise "competing" organizations. The last line of the Diaper Bank's Credo says it best:

"We can accomplish significant change if the whole community works together, focusing ALL the community's varied resources towards improving our community's quality of life. All the community must share ownership of our problems and our solutions."

What Do You Mean by "Asking Other Organizations for Help?"

Many organizational leaders almost choke when we suggest that their strongest allies could be other organizations - the ones they have been so used to considering their "competition." But the truth is that these other groups are passionate about the exact same things your organization's board and staff and volunteers are passionate about. If there are any groups who should know each other better, building the trust relationships that become friendships, it is all those other organizations you have viewed as your competition!

This is not pie in the sky. It is reality. We see others as "competition for scarce resources" when we see resources as scarce. And we hope this book has showed you that your organization's resources are anything but scarce - there is boundless potential for you to accomplish your mission in your community. The scarcity-based feeling one encounters in many nonprofit organizations is one of the stumbling blocks to making our communities amazing places to live. If your organization is driven to improve the quality of life in your community, one of the places to start will be at the heart of that scarcity mind-set.

Support for your mission is as abundant as the passionate chords you strike in your community. That passion is at the heart of what it takes to ensure your mission is one the community would not let die. And when we realize that and see it in action, we begin to realize the scarcity mind-set may not be the only way to see the world.

So this section is about going to that next step. We have provided strategies that allow beginners to put a toe in the water, as well as strategies that allow the more courageous to dive in completely. In either case, you will quickly begin to see that we are far stronger together than any of our organizations could ever be on its own.

The protective walls we have built around our organizations have kept out the very people who care passionately about the causes we care about. By taking a community engagement approach, we bust down those protective walls, inviting those whose passions we share into our home, to begin sharing ideas and thinking about the larger things we can accomplish together. From there, the gifts we provide to our communities - creating significant, visionary change in the community's quality of life - are truly without limit.

What is the Goal of This Strategy?

The goal of this strategy is the core of your mission. The goal is short term program effectiveness for those you serve, and long term improvement to the quality of life in our communities and our world. The goal is about learning together, exploring together, and leveraging the power nonprofit organizations often do not realize they have.

The goal is the whole reason you have joined your organization's board in the first place - to make a difference.

Who Will We Contact for This Strategy?

The target for this strategy are those people on your Life List who are involved in any way with another nonprofit organization in your community.

How Do We Ask Other Organizations for Help?

There are as many ways to engage other organizations as there are other organizations. The ways in which you will engage each other will be determined in part by the extent to which your missions mesh (Is one an environmental group, while yours is an arts group? Or are both organizations substance abuse treatment facilities?). Your engagement will also be determined by how deeply into this approach your board and staff are ready to go. Some may just want to dabble, to see how this approach feels to them. Others may want to dive in head first.

As with the other strategies in this book, we hope these ideas spark others, and that a Community Engagement approach becomes the culture at your organization.

STRATEGY #78 | Traveling Board Meetings

Probably one of the first toes your board can put in the water of learning and working with other organizations is to hold their board meetings at the facilities of organizations with whom you already have cooperative working relationships. At the end of the board meeting, set aside 15 minutes to have their Executive Director talk briefly about that other organization, perhaps sharing other opportunities for both groups to work together. And don't pass up the opportunity to tour their facility!

STRATEGY #79 | Program Discussions via a Focus Group Event

Using the approaches from Strategy #24, host a focus group event just for those who are active with other organizations doing similar work as your group is doing. As you review the information at Strategy #24, determine a good topic to share, and brainstorm questions you might ask that are forward-thinking, focused on what is exciting about the work you both do.

In addition, you might consider hosting a focus group for organizations whose work is only marginally related to the work you do, or whose work could perhaps enhance your own mission work if it were thought about differently. The mission of one of our clients was to train low income people to refurbish computers. The actual work combined job training with another mission - bridging the digital divide. Further, their work's eventual goal was to keep old computers (and their toxins) out of the landfills. Groups like the Sierra Club were a natural alliance they had never pursued. But a focus group event could make those alliances come alive.

STRATEGY #80 | Big Picture Discussions

For organizations doing the same work as your organization, nothing gets us past that sense of "competition" like focusing on the big picture: What long term impact do we want to have on our community 20 and 50 and 100 years from now? What impact could we have if we all worked together?

While in the short term, it may take some effort to get past that image of "organizations competing for scarce resources," when we ask those bigger picture questions - the ones at the heart of the very work we all do - all those day-to-day issues melt away. Instead of competitors, we more easily see ourselves as one single army, aimed at building a better place to live. And we begin to explore those possibilities together.

This type of discussion could be developed as an annual education forum on issues that are common to the boards and staff of all those organizations.

Or it could be developed as an annual Community Impact planning session, where those boards and staff come together to determine how they will jointly create big picture change in the issues they all care so passionately about.

Frequently, due to the different sorts of meetings that occur in the life of an Executive Director, EDs from organizations with similar missions have the opportunity to get to know each other. But it is rare that Board Members from those organizations gather to discuss these critical issues. There is so much both board and staff could learn from each other and accomplish together if they dedicate themselves to creating that structured environment, at least once a year.

The key to the success of this approach is that both board and staff attend, and that both board and staff from all those organizations see this as one of the most important points in each of their annual calendars - the sessions from which this group can link arms to create big picture change on behalf of your community.

STRATEGY #81 | A Day of Tours

One starting point for bringing together those organizations with similar missions could be a day devoted to touring a number of the facilities in town who are doing similar work. A joint committee of staff and boards from the various organizations might gather to arrange the day, and determine the types of information everyone would want to know from each other. (And the best way to determine those questions is to take 10 minutes at a board meeting to ask each of the boards what they would like to know!) How do you do your work? What is similar? What can we learn from the way others do their mission work? What results would we like to come out of this learning together?

STRATEGY #82 | **Individual Tours**

As your Board Members consider Strategy #11 - taking new friends on a tour - they may consider taking a friend who is a Board Member of another organization, precisely because he/she *is* a Board Member of another organization. "We have so much we can learn from each other. Could I tour you around our facility, so we can talk about the possibilities?"

Again, these might be individuals whose affiliation is closely aligned to your organization's work, or individuals where the connection is less obvious. "I have a sense there is a way our arts group and your historic preservation group can be working together. I have no idea what the possibilities are, but I would love to show you our facility, and perhaps see your facility, to explore some ideas together."

After touring your facility, be sure to follow up, as suggested in Strategy #11. And be sure part of that follow-up is a tour of your friend's organization!

What is the Role of the Board Member in this Strategy?

The role of the Board Member will first be to connect with those people on your Life Lists who are active in other organizations. Secondly, though, and almost more importantly, the job of the Board Member will be to attend, to participate, to learn, and to be willing to explore from a spirit of abundant possibility and potential, rather than the fear bred from the perception of competition for scarce resources. This is the highest calling of a Board Member - to actively work to make the community a better place to live.

AT THE DIAPER BANK

We spent a year doing the Community Sleuthing that led to creating the Diaper Bank in Phoenix. Over the course of that year, we spoke with funders and government representatives, nonprofit Executive Directors and Board Members, business people and volunteers. We shared with them the collaborative approach the Diaper Bank had been built upon in Tucson, and we talked about how much we hoped to prove that same collaborative approach could work anywhere.

And from virtually every person we spoke with, we heard almost the identical refrain: "I don't want to rain on your parade, but this will never work here. Organizations in the Valley do not work together." It was the rare person who did not wish us all sorts of luck on the one hand, while simultaneously adding that pessimistic, competition-tinged farewell.

Because one of the things that makes the Diaper Bank so powerful is precisely that it is built upon a model of shared resources, shared mission, and shared responsibility for improving the community's quality of life, we knew the whole mission would change if we changed those very basic assumptions. We were therefore even more determined to see if perhaps what we were hearing was more assumption than fact.

So after a year of sleuthing, we held our breath and dove into the deep end, convening the Diaper Bank's first "organizing" meeting. We announced the meeting to those with whom we had met throughout the year and sent press releases through the local newspapers and networking groups.

75 people showed up at that first organizational meeting. After a brief talk about the purpose of the project, they broke into committees, and enthusiastically went to work.

continued☞

AT THE DIAPER BANK (continued)

After a year of hearing that same message, over and over - "the organizations here will never work together" - we were skeptical about the group's initial enthusiasm. Could this momentum continue? Will these groups continue to work together to build something that has never existed in Phoenix before?

History has proven that the answer was, of course, "yes." And history also proved what we knew to be true - that given the opportunity to share what they had in abundance - knowledge and experience and skills - these organizations would stop seeing each other as competition, and instead work together to create a resource they would all eventually share.

Meetings were hosted at a different agency each time. At the end of each meeting, the host would spend a few moments talking about his/her organization and then give a tour for those who were interested. After just a few sessions, when it came time to decide where the next meeting would be held, hands would shoot into the air - everyone wanted to show off the work they were doing!

But the flip side of that was true as well. Those who attended those meetings were just as eager to take those tours and learn about the work being done by others. The participant from one tiny organization summed it up best, after touring one of the area's highest profile (and highest budget) organizations. "We do similar work, but on a much smaller scale. We don't even have a big enough meeting room to host one of these meetings! I have always wanted to see how they do things here, but I never would have had the nerve to ask if I could visit if it weren't for this opportunity."

From the synergy of working together to draft Requests for Proposals and other Diaper Bank-related work, and further from the synergy of learning from each other and seeing each other's facilities, all sorts of collaborative ideas, completely unrelated to the Diaper Bank, began to emerge. (Dimitri and I began to realize that instead of noticing the excitement of that collaborative spark, we were beginning to take greater notice of those rare meetings where there was no spark!)

We all know how the story ends. Those funders and government leaders and others "in the know" who suggested the Valley's agencies would not work together were clearly wrong. Leaders from over 50 organizations built the Diaper Bank in the Phoenix metro area, and they continue to work together - helping when there are diapers to sort and distribute, doing Diaper Drives, sending volunteers.

When there was something to be gained that was grander than any one organization could address; when the benefit was so clear, for both the community overall, and for each of their clients independently, these organizations with such a strong reputation for NOT working together were an amazing team. They set aside their own needs for the greater good. (We often heard the refrain, "If we wind up with only 10 packages of diapers, that will be 10 packages we didn't have when we started.")

We are what we think. If we think we are competitors, we throw up those walls and the community is the one to lose out in the end. When we realize we are all in this together, building *one* community, with *one* shared mission - the mission of making life better - it is astounding what we can *and do* accomplish.

Brainstorm Sheet: _____

❖ Asking Other Nonprofit Organizations for Help

What big picture topics would your organization love to tackle, if you had an army of other organizations working by your side?

1.) _____
2.) _____
3.) _____
4.) _____
5.) _____
6.) _____

What educational opportunities would be beneficial to all the organizations who care about the same issues?

1.) _____
2.) _____
3.) _____
4.) _____
5.) _____
6.) _____

What could all the organizations who care about your organization's mission learn from touring each other's facilities? What could be the benefits of such tours for your Board Members?

1.) _____
2.) _____
3.) _____
4.) _____
5.) _____
6.) _____

Friendship is the only cement that
will ever hold the world together.

Woodrow Wilson

PART 4

To Make a Friend Be a Friend

The only reward of virtue is virtue; the only way to have a friend
is to be one.

Ralph Waldo Emerson

STEP 4 # To Make a Friend, Be a Friend

This section is last but absolutely not least. It is so "not least" that we considered making it the first section, rather than the last. Instead, we decided to make it the period at the end of the very long sentence that is this book.

If the board is the natural link to the community - the community to whom your organization is accountable, the community for whom your organization is providing the benefit you provide - then this is the section where the board's rubber meets the road.

Among a board's other jobs, its position at the top of the organizational chart means the board is the role model for the Executive Director, for the rest of the staff, for the volunteers, and for the community. If the individuals who are ultimately accountable for every action and inaction on the part of the organization - the Board Members - do not act like true friends to the organization, supporting the organization in every way they can imagine, why should anyone else?

None of the steps in this section are any more onerous than the strategies in the rest of the book. The difference is that while we suggest you try a few of those other strategies a time, the strategies in this section are ones that every single Board Member should be doing - your whole board doing all these strategies.

These seven simple actions will make such a marked difference in supporting your organization's mission, you will be inspired to see what else your board can accomplish. And once you have taken these steps yourselves, you will be energized to encourage others to become friends and do the same.

The last strategy is one that no one can do but the board. It is about accountability for what matters. It is about the very essence of not only your organization, but the community all your efforts are aimed at impacting. If you implement none of the other strategies in this book, and only implement #89, your organization will be well on the road to engaging your community in building a better place to live.

There is no better gift of friendship any Board Member can give to the community he or she loves than to aim at making that community a better place to live for everyone.

Strategies in this section include:

#83 - #88	To Make Friend, Be a Friend
#89	Governing for Impact

To Make a Friend, Be a Friend

How can we in good conscience ask others to do what we have not done ourselves? The Diaper Bank's Board Members remind me continually that while this is common sense, it is not as common as we would hope.

And here is how they remind me: As they worked to create the document that explains to prospective Board Members what will be expected of them, Board Members talked about how different this board is from others they sit on. "We are expected to pitch in on this board - to volunteer, to make connections, to bring diapers to board meetings. On so many other boards, I am expected to simply attend meetings. This board expects me to set an example."

The result of this? The board feels connected to the organization in so many ways. Being on this board has become a big part

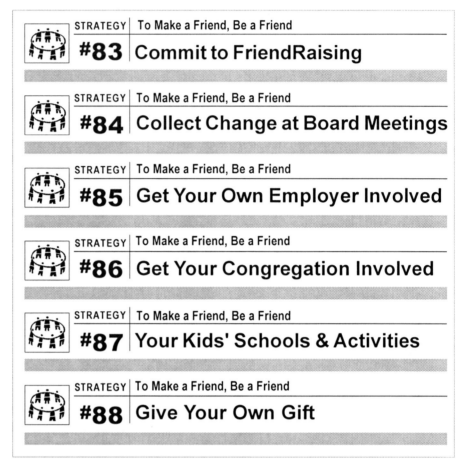

	STRATEGY	To Make a Friend, Be a Friend
	#83	**Commit to FriendRaising**
	STRATEGY	To Make a Friend, Be a Friend
	#84	**Collect Change at Board Meetings**
	STRATEGY	To Make a Friend, Be a Friend
	#85	**Get Your Own Employer Involved**
	STRATEGY	To Make a Friend, Be a Friend
	#86	**Get Your Congregation Involved**
	STRATEGY	To Make a Friend, Be a Friend
	#87	**Your Kids' Schools & Activities**
	STRATEGY	To Make a Friend, Be a Friend
	#88	**Give Your Own Gift**

of who each of those Board Members is. At the Diaper Bank, the Board Members are truly the organization's best friends.

What Is This Strategy About?

This strategy is about the Golden Rule. We cannot ask others to do what we are not willing to do ourselves.

The Goal of this Strategy

The goal of this strategy is to combine all the goals of all the strategies in this book, and then some.

More than anything, the goal is community engagement. Setting an example. Walking the talk.

Being a true friend.

Who is the Target for this Strategy?

Your Board Members. Period.

How to Do This Strategy

If you can guide others to do these things, you can do them yourselves - and should.

STRATEGY #83 | ## Commit to FriendRaising

Adding FriendRaising to the expectations for Board Members is more than just giving lip service to the importance of Community Engagement. Done right, this will be a policy that will be written into the letter of commitment signed by each Board Member, and their performance as a Board Member will be measured against that commitment.

We have worked with boards who have set as policy that each Board Member will introduce at least X number of new friends per year to the organization. We have worked with boards who have been more specific, setting as policy that each Board Member will link the organization with at least one speaking opportunity per year. The decision about how strict to make your policy is up to your board. But if you are committed to raising friends and engaging with the community at a meaningful level, put that in the form of a written policy, add it to your board's letter of commitment, and measure to ensure Board Members are walking that talk.

 STRATEGY #84 | ## Collect Change at Board Meetings

Keep a big glass jar just for the board to empty its change at every meeting - board meetings, committee meetings. If you do this at every meeting, you will build this activity into the very culture of the board. New Board Members will not even ask - they will just join in. This ritual levels the playing field, as all Board Members, rich and poor, can give something, feeling good about it as the pennies add up.

These small, almost insignificant amounts add up more quickly than you might think, and they are a great way to keep the board in the spirit of supporting the organization.

STRATEGY #85 | ## Get Your Own Employer Involved

Looking at all the options in Strategies #49 through #53, work with your employer to see how your company and its employees can get involved.

STRATEGY #86 | ## Get Your Own Congregation Involved

As noted in Strategies #68 through #73, the best liaison from your organization to any congregation is someone who is already a member of that congregation. If you are active in your congregation, find out how your congregation can become a friend.

STRATEGY #87 | ## Get Your Kids' Schools and Other Activities Involved

Strategies #57 through #67 have all kinds of ideas about how your organization can benefit from the kindness of children. Your own kids are a great place to start! When you show them about giving back, about becoming a friend to others who need their help, you are also sharing with your family a part of your life that is typically "adults only." Your kids may know you go to board meetings, but involving them encourages them to understand what that really means, engaging them in the mission you care about.

STRATEGY #88 | ## Give Your Own Gift

It cannot be said any more simply than that. Write that check. And make it generous.

This is not about raising money. It is about being a credible friend.

This is an issue many boards struggle with: Should Board Members be required to give dollars in addition to their time and their connections?

The answer is a definitive "yes." Board Members need to give more than just their time. They need to give money to the organization. They need to donate cash at a level that is generous, regardless of how much time they already donate, and regardless of their financial means. The amount should be personal and left up to each Board Member, because at every level of the financial scale, there is a cash donation that Board Member would consider to be generous for his/her means.

Before you start to argue that giving of your time should negate your need to also give money; before you start to argue that getting others to give should count against what you give yourself - listen to reason:

Imagine your Executive Director addressing a prospective major donor:

Donor: "Has every member of your board given to the organization?"

ED: "Well some give time, while others give money. And some introduce us to others who give, which we count against their own giving."

Donor: "Well I give my time to the organization - you know that. And I got you that foundation grant last year from our local corporation. So if the people who lead your organization - your Board Members - don't feel it is important enough to give their own dollars in addition to getting others to give or volunteering their time, why should I give?"

SAMPLE BOARD GIVING POLICY

Here is a sample Board Giving policy that no Board Member should have a problem with:

Each Board Member will make an annual gift to the organization, to the best of his/her means, at a level he/she feels is generous.

(Thanks to Jeane Vogel of Fundraising Innovations for the "at a level he/she feels is generous" part. We have used that kicker ever since we saw it in one of Jeane's newsletters, and boards take to it really well!)

It is important not to set a dollar amount in this policy. There are a number of reasons for this.

- A board we worked with had a $250 annual giving requirement, and each Board Member gave $250. A few of those Board Members, however, had significant giving capability. Because they were only asked to give $250 per year, that is what they gave. When that board switched to this policy, two of those Board Members increased their gifts to $1,000 each.

- We have also worked with boards that required a given number of board seats be filled by clients who received the service - folks of very little means. In one case, a struggling single mom gave $1.00 and wept as she did so, telling the ED that she had never been asked to give before, and that she had always felt she was "less than" the other Board Members, because they gave and she felt she could not.

So do not set a dollar amount. Let Board Members give to the best of their means, at a level each feels is generous. You will raise money, you will raise credibility, and you will raise enthusiasm among your Board Members, as they show by example that generosity is at the heart of true friendship.

Again, this is a matter of friendship - of the credibility that comes with walking your talk, and not asking someone to do something you have not done yourself.

Now imagine this scenario:

George: Hey Susan, will you help my brother move out of his apartment this weekend? He could sure use your truck, and you and your husband are in such good shape - between your muscle and your truck, it would be a great help.

Susan: We're happy to help. Shall we pick you up, or should we just meet there?

George: Oh I'm not going to be there - I really value my weekends. That's why I'm asking you to do it!

Ridiculous? How is that any different from what we expect if we are asking friends to help when we have chosen not to?

If a board is to be seen as credible to its friends, it is essential that 100% of the board give of their dollars - each to their means, at a level each Board Member feels is generous. It builds credibility, but even more than that, it gets to the heart of being a true friend. (For a sample board giving policy, see the box to the left.)

What is the Role of the Board Member in this Strategy?

The role of the Board Member in this activity? Walk the talk! Get involved, give of yourself, and support the organization you are leading.

Be a true friend.

AT THE DIAPER BANK

Because the Diaper Bank started as Dimitri and my "baby," sometimes it is hard for us to realize how big it has become. For us, the Diaper Bank is like the child who grows up to be the head of state of a great nation, whose parents still think of him as the kid playing kickball in the yard. He's not a world leader, he's my kid!

And so, when one of our founding Board Members came to me early in her board tenure and told me, "I've asked my attorney to rewrite my will, to include the Diaper Bank," I literally welled up and cried. Someone cared about my baby so much that they were willing to give such an important gift!

But here's the more important part of the story. That Board Member's gift made me realize that in all the years the Diaper Bank had been part of our lives, I had not changed my will to include the Diaper Bank in my own will! Imagine forgetting your own child like that! But truly, it had never occurred to me - we had talked about it for everyone else, and when it came to my own will - well that old piece of paper had been stuck in a drawer for so long, I had never even thought about it!

That is why, from our own first-hand experience, we now ask organizations who are urging donors to place the organization in their wills, "Before you ask others to do this, have you done so yourself?" From making donations, to making connections, to yes, including the organization in your will, if the board does not walk the talk, how can you ask others to do so?

#89 | Govern for Community Impact

We saved the most critical strategy for last, because it has to do with the very essence of why your organization exists. Focus the board's efforts on this strategy, and the community will not let your mission work die.

That strategy is simple:

Make your organization a true friend to the community
by focusing your board's primary accountability on making your community a better place.

Your board's position at the top of the organizational chart means the buck stops with your board. That is the essence of accountability. And because an organization is accountable for providing the community with what it has promised to provide, the essence of building an organization the community would not let die is to live up to that promise. That means keeping your eye on the ball - community impact - and making sure the most talked about item at your board table is creating that incredible impact for your community.

If you aim for that level of impact, the rest - the money, the ethics, the systems - will all fall into place, because you simply cannot create that impact without it.

And if you aim for that level of impact, you will soon see that you cannot achieve it if the whole community is not part of your efforts. That is the imperative behind your board's community engagement efforts.

If the organization is doing amazing things for the community, all the strategies in this book become easy to do, because you do not have to go out of your way to prove your organization is a true friend to the community. As your board works to ensure the community is receiving the very most benefit possible today, the community will know that.

And as your board works to ensure the community of the future - the community of your grandchildren and their grandchildren - is a better place, tomorrow and the tomorrow after that, the community will know that as well. The evidence will be everywhere, and the community would not dream of living without the work you are doing.

That conscious focus on creating community impact is at the heart of being a Community-Driven organization, governed by a Community-Driven board.

The core philosophies that guide the Community-Driven approach are as true for your organization as they would be for your closest friends and your family.

Link arms to build a healthy, resilient, thriving community,
and the community will respond with love and friendship in return.

Hold a true friend with both your hands.

Nigerian Proverb

AfterWords

Friendship is a strong and habitual inclination in two persons to promote the good and happiness of one another.

Eustace Budgell

AfterWords

It would take many volumes to include an in-depth look at every topic discussed in this book. For that reason, we are providing two sources of information, to help you learn more about some of those topics.

First, we have created a FriendRaising Web Resource Area on our website, just for purchasers of this book.

Secondly, you will find information right here, in the AfterWords.

If there are topics you do not find covered here, that you feel would be helpful as you dive into your organization's FriendRaising activities, we hope you will let us know.

Help 4 NonProfits Website:
FriendRaising Web Resource Area

To add more in-depth information about some of the topics mentioned in this book, we have created a FriendRaising Web Resource Area at the Help 4 NonProfits website. If you found a topic in the main text of this book that interested you to learn more, that is what the Web Resource Area is all about.

As new items come to our attention, we will add that information to that FriendRaising Web Resource Area. We hope you will also let us know what additional information would be helpful as you navigate the approaches in this book.

In addition to information about many of the topics discussed here, you will also find downloadable PDFs of all the Brainstorm Sheets from the book, provided for your ease in printing them. We meant it when we said we want you to use this book as a workbook, scribbling in it and using it to think things through. And sometimes the only way to do that is to have more copies of the forms!

The FriendRaising Web Resource Area is exclusively for users of our FriendRaising workbook and is not accessible from our regular website. You will find the site at:

http://www.help4nonprofits.com/cgi-bin/register/locked.cgi

Because this Resource Area is exclusively for users of the workbook, when you arrive there for the first time, you will be asked to create a user name and password. From there, you will have full access to all the information at the FriendRaising Web Resource Area.

There is no charge for accessing the FriendRaising Web Resource Area. We see it as a way to extend what we have provided in this book, giving us the ability to add new information as we find it, to help with your FriendRaising efforts. So be sure to bookmark that page!

Shared Resources
(And More About the Diaper Banks)

As has been mentioned throughout this book, both Diaper Banks were built on a base of shared resources. By building these organizations in a way that was intended from the start to be cooperative, that model has laid the building blocks for the deep engagement the Diaper Banks have felt from their very first days.

Sharing resources does not have to happen only at the beginning of a project or program. At any point in the life of a program, you can assess the program's needs (as described in Strategy #3) and ask, "Who else in town is already doing this?"

The following are functions every program will likely need to address in some way or another, and some ways both Diaper Banks have shared those efforts with others in the community.

Function	How the Diaper Bank Shared Resources
Personnel	By collaborating with other social service providers to provide diapers to people in need, the Diaper Bank did not need to hire caseworkers. By collaborating on the warehousing side, the Diaper Bank did not need to hire warehouse staff.
Facilities	Both Diaper Banks share warehousing space that is owned by other organizations, and in both cases those situations were uncovered through an RFP process. In Tucson, the warehousing function is handled by Beacon Group, an organization serving the vocational needs of the disabled. In Phoenix, warehousing is provided by St. Mary's Food Bank.
Equipment	During December Diaper Drive, delivery vehicles are at a premium, as schools and businesses collect thousands of diapers to be picked up and brought to the warehouse. A local company that delivers free newspapers to supermarkets stepped up: "We not only have trucks all over town, but we have a dispatcher. When a school needs to have diapers picked up, just give them our number. Our dispatcher will get a truck to them!"
Administrative Support	During their start-up years, both Diaper Banks were under the fiscal sponsorship of Carondelet Foundation. This minimized the need for bookkeeping staff, as well as the need for annual audits, as the minimal dollars it took to run these programs were incorporated in the Foundation's audit.
Outreach to Clients	The Diaper Bank realized early on that our whole program could be used as outreach for those who are hard to reach with services, for example, undocumented residents. While timid about seeking service for themselves, it has been a different story when it comes to taking care of their babies. Therefore, early in its history, the Diaper Bank began partnering with organizations who could help these families with their other needs, once they had come to the Diaper Bank for assistance as that first step.

These are just some of the functions your programs might be able to share with others. The FriendRaising Web Resource Area at Help4NonProfits.com has additional information both about the Diaper Bank, and about approaches to sharing resources - part of taking a more Community-Driven approach to the work your organization is doing. (For access information to that secure site, turn to page 196)

Board Member Letter of Commitment & the Board Attendance Matrix

Letter of Commitment

The only way your board can hold board members to the commitments they have made - whether that is the commitment to donate to the organization, or simply to show up for meetings - is to have a document that outlines your expectations. That is why many boards require that Board Members sign a commitment letter, formally accepting the responsibility of governing the organization.

A sample letter of commitment can be found in our workbook, "Board Recruitment and Orientation: A Step-by-Step, Common Sense Guide."

For purposes of FriendRaising, at least two items should be included in your Letter of Commitment. The first is the commitment to make an annual cash donation to the organization, per Strategy #88. The second is the commitment to introduce at least X number of friends to the organization every year. The number of friends to be introduced is up to you, but the best way to ensure you are always engaging new friends is to require at least some level of introductions annually.

In addition to those two items, your organization may want to add a third FriendRaising commitment to that letter - the commitment to arrange for at least one speaking gig per year, regardless of the size of the audience. This is not the commitment to actually be the one to speak, but simply to arrange for that opportunity.

And lastly, you may want to include in those commitments some mechanism for Board Members to give thanks, whether that is to show up at your organization's office X times per year to make calls, or to write X Thank You notes.

Board Attendance Matrix

Depending on what your board requires of its board members, a simple chart can track those requirements. A sample matrix, covering the items noted above, is located at the FriendRaising Web Resource Area at Help4NonProfits.com (for access information to that secure site, turn to page 196).

Using a board attendance matrix, your board can easily monitor which of your board members may need a reminder or two.

Movies for Your Cause

As I was writing the section on movies, I asked friends and colleagues for suggestions of movies that might help one cause or another. The list became so exhaustive that we quickly realized that virtually every topic in the world has been addressed by at least one good movie.

The following is a partial list of movies you might use for a movie night. For a more comprehensive listing, head to the FriendRaising Web Resource Area at Help4NonProfits.com (for access information to that secure site, turn to page 196).

 ## Global Concerns:
Bandit Queen
Hotel Rwanda
Kundun
Life and Debt

 ## Social Service / Health Issues:
A Beautiful Mind
Iris
One Flew Over the Cuckoo's Nest
Patch Adams
Philadelphia
Rage Against the Darkness

 ## Social Issues:
Bread and Roses
Cider House Rules
Citizen Ruth
Color Purple
Crash
Hidden in America
Inherit the Wind
Norma Rae
Shawshank Redemption
To Kill a Mockingbird

Education:
Dangerous Minds
Finding Forrester
Inherit the Wind
School of Rock
Stand and Deliver
To Sir with Love

Arts:
Mad Hot Ballroom
Mr. Holland's Opus
Music of the Heart
OT: Our Town

Environment:
Erin Brockovich
Gorillas in the Mist
Winged Migration
Silkwood

The categories listed above are broad and you might disagree with where I have listed something or what I called the category. As I found in trying to list just this handful of examples, categorizing movies by theme is not an easy task, simply because a single movie might aim at making several different points. We hope you will use this list, as well as the further list at the FriendRaising Web Resource Area, as starting points to spark your own thinking. And please, send us suggestions for movies you think should be included!

The Power of Public Speaking

In Strategies #27-30, we mention that many books have been written about public speaking. Our favorites are listed at the FriendRaising Web Resource Area at Help4NonProfits.com (for access information to that secure site, turn to page 196).

Public Speaking is one of the most effective ways to build your army of friends and engage the community in your work. However, as we looked at the resources available to help nonprofit leaders use speaking to their organization's advantage, we found there were plenty of books on being an effective "public speaker" in a general sense, but nothing about developing a public speaking campaign to generate support for a nonprofit mission. There was nothing about deciding which stories to use, or what to leave the group as take-away information - the kinds of things specific to the needs of nonprofits.

There are also issues nonprofit leaders face as speakers that others usually do not have to worry about. For example, if you are at a Rotary or other function, and you are told not to ask for anything, how can you ask for something without it seeming like you are asking? (For us it has always been diapers!). Or if you are at a cocktail party, using your "Personal Advocacy" approach, how can you make sure you hit all your key points without boring your new friend to tears?

So we wrote a handbook on the subject - "Building Support Through Public Speaking: Tips, Tools and Secrets Any Nonprofit Leader Can Master."

If your organization is going to be using public speaking as a way to raise friends and engage the community with your mission, you will find our workbook and the other books at the FriendRaising Web Resource Area to be helpful guides for those efforts.

A Direct Mail Tip

In Strategies #75 and #76, we discussed using your fundraising appeals as a way to raise friends as well. As you consider the power direct mail has to raise both funds and friends, the FriendRaising Web Resource Area has great books and other resources regarding the fundraising aspects of direct mail.

There is one tip we did want to offer here, though, as it is a simple thing that can increase the dollar results of your direct mail appeal. It relates to the donor envelope you include with your mailing. And like the FriendRaising strategies in this book, it is an approach we learned through trial and error.

To encourage donors to increase the size of their gift, print the gift range on your donor envelope in descending order. For example:

☐ $2,500 ☐ $1,000 ☐ $500 ☐ $250 ☐ $100

I am sure there are fundraising gurus who could explain the psychology of why this works, but over the years, we found that when we reversed the order, more donors increased their gifts.

The FriendRaising Web Resource Area at Help4NonProfits.com (for access information to that secure site, turn to page 196) will provide additional resources to help you with your direct mail and other campaigns, especially as you aim to make those efforts more asset-based, building your base of community support.

A Tip Worth Its Weight in Gold

We would be remiss if we did not recommend Charity Channel as a resource for your organization's staff and board.

Charity Channel is the world's largest online community of those working and volunteering in work related to creating community benefit. At Charity Channel you will find over 50 discussion groups, all related to the work we in the voluntary sector do every day. There is a discussion group related to Board issues, another related to Grants, another related to Human Resource issues. There is a forum for consultants to nonprofits and NGO's, and several forums for attorneys specializing in the law related to those organizations. Planned giving. Annual appeals and general fundraising. Accountability issues. If there is an area of this sector that interests you, you will find people from around the world to talk with about those issues through Charity Channel.

Charity Channel is a place to ask questions, to air concerns, to connect with others who do the same work you do - whether you are a staff person, a board member, a volunteer or a funder. Charity Channel will provide you with great information and discussions, every day via your email.

It is an amazing way to learn.

Lurk or participate. Ask or answer or just watch. Charity Channel has been hailed by the best in our profession as being the single most important source of ongoing education. If you are a Board Member, an Executive Director, a volunteer, an employee, a donor - or if your work is helping those in the voluntary sector as a consultant or attorney - you owe it to yourself to check out this incredible resource.

For more information, head to www.CharityChannel.com

The Sound a Thank You Makes

The following is from our website at www.Help4NonProfits.com. It has been a favorite article among fans of our site ever since it first appeared in 2003. We could not think of a better way to end this book than including it here, for you to enjoy as well.

The Sound a Thank You Makes

It was a crazy week - one of those weeks where I started working at 5am every morning, and fell into bed exhausted at 11pm every night, only to start at 5:00 the next morning.

As the founder of a tiny organization, when the Executive Director (our only full time employee) resigned, it was left to me to "mind the store" until a replacement could be found. So, for the first time since founding the Diaper Bank some years ago, I had become its Interim Executive Director. And as luck would have it, I stepped into the position at the most hectic time of year - the celebration of our 10th Annual December Diaper Drive, a month-long series of events to raise 1 million diapers for those in need.

With the turmoil of the ED's departure, we were 2 weeks late getting our annual mailing out. We were a week behind in arranging for our Big Event. There was a grant deadline we had just learned about. And of course, there were all the normal day-to-day things of running a nonprofit organization.

Friday afternoon at 4:00, I finished the last deadline. I let out the kind of breath that lets you know you haven't taken a real breath in quite some time.

With our part-time staff and our volunteers in the other room putting the finishing touches on the mailing, I couldn't very well say, "I'm exhausted. I'm going home!" After all, they had been working just as hard as I had all week.

So I started to sort the stack of mail that had accumulated on my desk during my week of insanity. Bills. Donations. Invitations. Junk.

And it is the next thing I did that saved my whole day, my whole week. It is that one simple action that I recommend to you - not just because it is the right thing to do, but because it feels so good.

I went through that stack of donation envelopes, and I called every person who gave, thanking them for their gift.

This is nothing new for me. Since stepping into this position, as soon as a donation arrives, I have called to thank every donor, no matter how small the gift. It takes a few minutes every day, and mostly I end up leaving messages, but that's ok. I've always felt it's just the right thing to do. If someone does something nice for you, you thank them. If nothing else, it's simply common courtesy.

continued ☞

It had been a whole week since I'd touched the mail - mail from our annual campaign. The stack was high. I started dialing.

Because the Diaper Drive gets a lot of publicity here in Tucson, many of the checks were for $5 and $10. You could tell from the names on the checks - Ella, Gertrude, Olivia - and from the shaky writing, that these checks were from elderly folks, probably on fixed incomes. I know their $5 is dear to them, and they are usually the first ones I call.

I had made a number of calls before I got to Mrs. Fontaine. Her phone rang and rang. When she finally picked up, it was clear she was having trouble breathing. I pictured her struggling to get to the phone, and I thought to myself, "Oh great. She has taken all her energy, thinking this is an important call, and it's just me calling to say thank you." I felt guilty for bothering her.

"Is this Mrs. Fontaine?" I said.

"Yes."

"Mrs. Fontaine, this is Hildy from the Diaper Bank. We received your donation, and I just wanted to thank you."

Mrs. Fontaine was not happy. Clearly she thought I was calling to solicit her, probably to ask for more money. I don't blame her - that's probably how I would react if any charity I ever gave to thought to call and thank me. (Hint - no charity I have ever given to has EVER called to thank me. Not one.)

I continued. "Your gift means a lot to us, and I really just wanted you to know that it will help a lot of people."

"But I only sent you $5!" I could hear her move from anger to confusion, but clearly she was softening up.

"But every penny counts!" I told her. "We just really appreciate your helping out, and I just wanted you to know that."

Now her voice was positively warm, surprised, happy. "Well thank you. Really it is so nice of you to call. How very very nice!" They say you can hear a smile over the phone, and I heard hers, loud and clear.

Mrs. Fontaine put me on a roll. I dialed with a fever. I forgot about the week behind me, a week where the sheer size of the mountain of work had overshadowed the reasons we were doing the work in the first place. I listened to donor after donor tell me what amazing things we are doing, and how they wish they could give us more. I heard THEM thanking ME, telling me how they appreciated what we do, encouraging us to keep it up, telling me how important it is.

continued ☞

Finally, the last call - a $200 VISA charge. From the sound of the voice at the other end of the phone, this was a professional woman my own age. And from the moment I started the call, she acted as if she had been chosen for the Publisher's Clearinghouse Sweepstakes! "I can't believe you are calling me! This is so nice, so unexpected! You have a wonderful weekend!" she told me over and over in the short time of the call.

I left the office with a smile on my face. Yes, I was exhausted, and yes, my bed felt great.

But I had found a joy I never expected as I thought about clearing my desk. It wasn't the joy of finishing the job, or getting through the pile. It wasn't even the joy of remembering why we do the work we do.

It was the joyful sound a Thank You makes when it lands.

And so,
for the sake of your own organization's health,
and for the sake of finding a bit of joy in your own day,
pick up the phone.
Say "Thank You."

And listen to the sound that Thank You makes
when it lands in the hearts of your friends.

About the Author

Hildy Gottlieb is President and co-founder of Help 4 NonProfits & Tribes, an organization renowned for helping organizations provide more significant impact in their communities.

Photograph by Art Clifton AC Productions

Frustrated with classic "organizational development" tools that do little to help organizations create significant community impact (board development and governance models, strategic planning, fund development, marketing, etc.), Hildy and business partner Dimitri Petropolis spent years developing and testing their own methods. The result is an approach for building Community-Driven Organizations. The core philosophy behind the Community-Driven approach is simple:

The only way voluntary organizations will create significant improvement to the quality of life in our communities and our world is if all the work those organizations do - from programs to fundraising to governance and everything in between - is aimed at creating and sustaining that degree of community impact.

To help organizations become more Community-Driven, the Help 4 NonProfits & Tribes team has developed the Community-Driven Institute, providing educational programs to help organizations make the world a better place to live.

Hildy and Dimitri are the co-founders of Tucson's Southern Arizona Community Diaper Bank, the first organization in the U.S. focused entirely on providing this critical necessity to those in need. They are also the co-founders of the Valley of the Sun Community Diaper Bank in the Phoenix metropolitan area.

Hildy is the author of the best-selling "Board Recruitment and Orientation: A Step-by-Step, Common Sense Guide." She has written extensively in nonprofit and tribal publications, including the Chronicle of Philanthropy and Indian Country Today. The recipient of many awards, Hildy is proudest of two awards she and Dimitri received together: The inaugural Charity Channel Founder's Award for "Contributions to the professional excellence of their colleagues, and the philanthropic example they set"; and the Points of Light Presidential Citation they received from President Bill Clinton, for their efforts in building the Diaper Bank.

Outside her work life, Hildy is the single mother of a daughter in college who continues to be her inspiration. Hildy credits her abilities as a speaker to years of teaching Spanish and creative writing in her daughter's grade school classes.

To contact Hildy and to sign up for Help 4 NonProfits' e-newsletter, head to www.Help4NonProfits.com

The glory of friendship is not the outstretched hand, nor the kindly smile, nor the joy of companionship; it is the spiritual inspiration that comes to one when he discovers that someone else believes in him and is willing to trust him with his friendship.

Ralph Waldo Emerson

LaVergne, TN USA
23 November 2010
206076LV00001B/48/A

9 780971 448209